ON THE TRAIL
OF THE
ROYAL SCOT

ON THE TRAIL
OF THE
ROYAL SCOT

DAVID PACKER

THE HISTORY PRESS

First published in the United Kingdom in 2009 by
The History Press
The Mill, Brimscombe Port, Stroud, Gloucestershire, GL5 2QG

British Library Cataloguing in Publication Data
A catalogue record for this book is available from the British Library.

ISBN 978-0-7509-4625-4

Typeset in 10/12pt Palatino.
Typesetting and origination by
The History Press.
Printed and bound in England.

Contents

Introduction

O n the Trail of the Royal Scot is a book about the route and the history of the famous train. We see the 'Royal Scot' and other passenger and freight trains at many locations between the two termini at London Euston and Glasgow Central. Because it is, primarily, a pictorial account of this famous train and its route, the book does not pretend to provide an in-depth study but, rather, a celebratory reflection.

The route of the 'Royal Scot' has seen many changes over the years. Although there are old items of railway interest that can be still seen, such as mileposts and gradient markers, the passage of time has seen the loss of stations, semaphore signals, signal-boxes, railway sheds, sidings, level crossings and water tanks; all of which has changed the railway landscape.

At one time there were in excess of 120 stations, including those in north London used by local services only. Today, less than half survive. Surprisingly, more than two-thirds of the closures pre-date the Beeching era, the earliest closures being in the 1930s. Careful observation, preferably with the assistance of Ordnance Survey maps, may help to locate the position of some of the old stations. Typical clues would be a road bridge nearby, an approach road by the side of the railway and the track-bed of former sidings.

Very few of the old semaphore signals exist along the West Coast Main Line (WCML). At one time they could be seen as single arms, brackets and, as at Preston, an impressive array of signals stretching from one side of the line to the other. The signal-boxes that operated the signals have largely disappeared too, replaced by visually ugly power boxes, each one of which has replaced up to a hundred of the traditional boxes. A few redundant boxes may be spotted along the route together with those that have survived for a specific purpose, such as the manning of one of the rare level crossings, as at Hest Bank in Lancashire and a few in Scotland.

In the steam age there were at least twenty sheds along the journey but these have been replaced by a handful of modern traction depots that are barely noticeable. There are one or two surviving structures such as at Stafford and Carlisle Upperby and, of course, the oldest of all at Chalk Farm in London. One of the best-known sheds at Carnforth survives in railway use and boasts a coaling tower. The track-beds of former sidings and branches can often be made out, but all the water tanks, columns and water troughs (a London & North Western Railway invention) have disappeared.

As for the other landmarks, apart from the disappearance of the famous Euston arch at the beginning of the journey and of the old Wembley stadium, the main changes have been industrial. Factories have disappeared through the loss of industries or rationalisation. The chimneys of the brick-works near Bletchley, the engineering works at Rugby and Stafford, the coal industry around Nuneaton, Lancashire and Lanarkshire, the mills of Lancashire and the iron and steel industries around Wigan and Motherwell have all either reduced significantly or disappeared completely.

If the lineage of the 'Royal Scot' can be traced back to the nineteenth century then the route itself can claim a history that began at the dawn of the modern railway network with connections to the very first steam locomotives. Most travellers arriving at Euston will be unaware that in the vicinity of nearby Gower Street in 1808, Richard Trevithick gave a public demonstration of his second locomotive, the Catch Me Who Can. He had already built the very first steam locomotive in 1804. Coincidentally, his son, Francis Trevithick, became the first locomotive superintendent for the London & North Western Railway (LNWR) in 1846 at Crewe, the principal railway works along the WCML. The traveller from Euston, if using the forecourt directly in front of the station, may enter without noticing the statue of Robert Stephenson. He was the engineer in charge of building the railway from Euston to Birmingham that opened in 1838. However, his achievements, which include the building of the historic *Rocket*, extend well beyond those in connection with this railway. His stature can be gauged by the fact that he is buried in Westminster Abbey.

Robert's father, George Stephenson, achieved fame at the beginning of the railway era through his building of some of the earliest locomotives and of the Stockton & Darlington Railway. That fame was consolidated when, against the physical odds and much vocal opposition, he completed the Liverpool & Manchester Railway. He was involved with the extension to Birmingham but it was mainly Joseph Locke who carried out the work of the Grand Junction Railway. Likewise, it was Locke whose proposals were accepted to engineer a route from Lancaster to Carlisle via Shap in preference to George Stephenson's proposals to take the circuitous route around the Cumbrian coast.

The WCML was built in stages, the earliest sections being the oldest of all the principal main lines as they were extensions north and south from the historic Liverpool & Manchester Railway in the early 1830s. The Caledonian Railway's main line did not open until 1848. Until that time Anglo-Scottish trains along the West Coast route terminated at Fleetwood for the boat to Scotland. Unlike the main lines, which were constructed outwards from London, this railway spread from Lancashire. The Warrington & Newton Railway, just 4¼ miles long and who employed Robert Stephenson as engineer, opened in 1831. The 7-mile long Wigan Branch Railway, engineered by Charles Vignoles, opened in 1832. Both were operated initially by the Liverpool & Manchester Railway. The Grand Junction Railway then progressively extended a line from Warrington southwards to Birmingham, which was completed in 1837, while the North Union Railway opened their line from Wigan to Preston in 1838. Work on the London & Birmingham Railway took longer to complete with greater obstacles to overcome and was completed in 1838.

Meanwhile the route northwards from Preston was opened to Lancaster in 1840 (the Lancaster & Preston Junction Railway), and the difficult path through the hills to Carlisle followed Joseph Locke's proposals to follow the Lune Valley and then up to Shap Summit, thus avoiding the need for any tunnelling. Indeed, it is a surprising feature of this route that there are so few tunnels, and all of them south of Stafford. The completion of the Caledonian Railway's line from Carlisle to Glasgow was the last piece of the jigsaw, but that is not strictly correct because, subsequently, there have been two diversions. One of them was the building of a new line from Rugby to Stafford (the Trent Valley line) built to avoid congestion around Birmingham and speed up services to the north. The other was the bypassing of the Liverpool & Manchester Railway's section from Earlestown to Parkside by constructing a cut-off line between what is now Winwick Junction and Golborne Junction in 1864.

Before the WCML was completed throughout in its original form, the first rationalisation of railway companies had taken place with the Liverpool & Manchester Railway becoming part of the Grand Junction Railway in 1845. In turn, this was amalgamated with the London & Birmingham Railway to become the newly formed LNWR in 1846. The Lancaster & Carlisle Railway and the North Union Railway remained independent until 1879 and 1889 respectively while the whole route north of Carlisle continued to be operated by the Caledonian Railway.

The last section of the LNWR's route to Carlisle to pass into its ownership was the short stretch between Euxton Junction and Preston, which was jointly operated with the Lancashire & Yorkshire Railway. The two companies had a good working relationship and merged in 1922, just one year before the grouping of the many varied railway companies into four principal companies: the London Midland & Scottish Railway (LMS), the London & North Eastern Railway (LNER), Great Western Railway (GWR) and Southern Railway (SR). At this point the whole of the WCML came under the control of one company as the LMS inherited the locomotives, coaching and wagon stock, and infrastructure of various companies including the LNWR, Midland Railway (MR), North Staffordshire Railway (NSR), Lancashire & Yorkshire Railway (L&YR), Furness Railway (FR), Maryport & Carlisle Railway (M&C), Glasgow & South Western Railway (G&SWR) and the Caledonian Railway (CR), all of which had their own connections with the WCML. It is worth remembering that the GWR, North Eastern Railway (NER) and North British Railway (NBR) also ran services along parts of the WCML and these connections would continue almost to the end of the steam era at locations such as Crewe and Carlisle. A feature of the railways before the grouping was the wide variety of liveries belonging to the individual railway companies. Much of this individuality would be lost from 1923, to the regret, no doubt, of many a railway enthusiast of the time.

It took some years for the LMS to become a unified force and, on the locomotive front, this partly came about with the appointment of William A. Stanier (formerly of the GWR) as Chief Mechanical Engineer in 1932. During the Stanier era the romance returned to railways with powerful and fast express locomotives stirring up the interest of the public. Much of this was generated by the rivalry between the LMS and the LNER in the 1930s although the 'Royal Scot' train and locomotive contributed to this interest as a result of its trip to the USA and Canada in 1933. In retrospect, the LMS era was short; twenty-five years, of which six years were during wartime. However, some of the locomotives built during its lifetime would last to the end of steam and outlive those built by BR in the 1950s.

BR inherited a run-down network, and the Modernisation Plan of 1955 led to the introduction of widespread dieselisation in an attempt to produce efficiencies. The closures of lines and railway stations and other facilities became a feature of this era although the LMS had begun the process as early as the 1930s. The WCML was affected by the closure of wayside stations, firstly in the LMS era, then in the 1950s and again during the process of electrification – the single most important development of the line in the twentieth century. History repeated itself when, like the initial building of the line, electrification spread south from Manchester and Liverpool and was completed in 1966. A new Euston was opened in 1968 but it would be another six years before electrification to Glasgow would become reality and the Electric Scots would open a new chapter on 6 May 1974. This, together with track improvements, helped to bring train journey times down to 5 hours. Thirty years later and long after the abandonment of the Advanced Passenger Train that promised so much, the introduction of the tilting Pendolino trains have reduced scheduled times still further to under 4½ hours. However, as the 'Royal Scot' no longer features in the timetables as at the time of writing, it is worth moving on to consider a brief history of this train.

Brief History of the Royal Scot

The train known as the 'Royal Scot' ran for the first time between London and Glasgow on 11 July 1927. In the same year the first of a new series of locomotives, known as the 'Royal Scot' class, was completed for the LMS. They were designed to haul the heaviest trains on the WCML including their namesake, the 10am departures from both London and Glasgow.

The 'Royal Scot' was only one of several trains that year to be named by the LMS. What was not new was the 10 a.m. departure. Except for a period during the First World War, there had been a train leaving Euston at 10 a.m. since 1862. When the WCML opened throughout in 1848 the journey time to Glasgow took 13½ hours, whereas the initial 'Royal Scot' service ran to a scheduled time of 8¼ hours.

The 10 a.m. express of the 1860s would have been hauled by 2–4–0s, often in pairs as required by the load. One of the most famous types of 2–4–0 was F.W. Webb's 'Precedent' class that worked the LNWR's main line trains for many years, and given its small size was capable of great feats of haulage when necessary. These locomotives were produced at a time when the 4–4–0s were becoming the standard express type of locomotive. The most famous of the 'Precedents' was the celebrated no. 790 *Hardwicke* which achieved lasting fame for its exploits in the 'Race to the North' in 1895. This name is given to a series of high-speed running between London and Aberdeen operated by the LNWR and CR on the west coast and GNR, NER and NBR on the east coast after the opening of the Forth Bridge in 1894. During one journey on 22 August 1895 *Hardwicke* hauled a train between Crewe and Carlisle, including the climb to Shap, at an average speed of 67.2 mph, a record that was only broken in November 1936 by Stanier's 'Princess Royal', no. 6201 *Princess Elizabeth*. Happily, *Hardwicke* was preserved and is part of the national collection.

By the 1890s the 4–4–0s were handling many of the express trains while the first design of 4–6–0s were appearing in small numbers. North of the border the 'Dunalastair' 4–4–0s proved very successful on express trains and when George Whale took over as CME of the LNWR in 1903 he, too, set about producing a simple 4–4–0 called the 'Precursors' from June 1904. They helped to reduce double-heading and improve punctuality. They could even handle 350–400-ton trains for various destinations including Glasgow. His 'Experiment' 4–6–0s were not as successful at first because of poor steaming, but his successor, Bowen-Cooke, improved both the 'Precursors' and the 'Experiments' by providing superheating. He also designed new 4–4–0s in the shape of 'George the Fifths' which became great performers, and the 'Prince of Wales' 4–6–0s.

In 1911, the Caledonian Railway produced the first of what were known as its 'Cardean' class of 4–6–0. They were used on the WCML between Glasgow and Carlisle hauling trains such as the 'corridor' (later the 'Mid-day Scot') and the train that would later become the 'Royal Scot'. These engines lasted until 1933. In 1913 Bowen-Cooke introduced the LNWR's first large express engine, the 4-cylinder 'Claughton' 4–6–0 which, together with his new 'Prince of Wales' 4–6–0s, handled the heaviest expresses. They continued to be built after the First World War but in 1920 Bowen-Cooke died and after the Grouping of 1923 the newly formed LMS conducted trials to test the capabilities of the various express locomotives in their ownership.

However, in the mid-1920s, as loads increased, there was a need for more powerful engines at short notice on the WCML. A GWR 'Castle' was borrowed for trials in 1926 and the results showed that a locomotive of similar power was required for the line. The need for larger engines had become urgent and so Henry Fowler (who had succeeded George Hughes as CME of the LMS) attempted to obtain the drawings for the 'Castle' from Swindon but without success. However, the SR provided drawings of their new 'Lord Nelsons'. In the event the new design borrowed a little from the 'Lord Nelson', from the 'Castle' and from Fowler's own 2–6–4 tanks that were about to be produced at Derby. With the drawings complete, problems were then encountered in building the new locomotives as the main railway works at Crewe, Derby, Horwich and St Rollox (Glasgow) were fully occupied. Help came from the North British Locomotive Company in Glasgow who, in remarkably quick time, produced the first fifty of the new engines by the end of 1927.

The first 'Royal Scots' emerged in August, after the inauguration of the new 'Royal Scot' express service from 11 July 1927. Initially, the train was a non-stop service with an engine change at Carnforth No. 2 box and a division of the Glasgow and Edinburgh portions at Symington. The train was worked by double-headed combinations, typically a 'Claughton' and 'George the Fifth' to Carnforth and a pair of Midland 4–4–0 Compounds to Glasgow. However, the winter timetables saw the beginning of non-stop working to Carlisle from Euston using 'Royal Scots', claiming the British record for daily non-stop running.

Workings with these locomotives began officially on 26 September, with no. 6100 on the Down train and no. 6104 on the Up, making the journey on the 'Royal Scot' the longest non-stop run at 299¼ miles. The average speed to Carlisle was 52mph but the focus at that time was on punctuality in order to gain public confidence. The fifteen-coach load was reduced to twelve coaches outside the summer timetable except during peak holiday times.

At the inception of the 1928 summer timetable, the 'Royal Scot' became a non-stop service to Glasgow in the timetables. However, for operational purposes, the northbound train was booked to stop at Carlisle Kingmoor instead of Citadel while the Up working was booked to stop at Carlisle No. 12 box, south of Citadel station. Prior to the commencement of the new timetable, the 'Royal Scot' gained memorable publicity as a result of two non-stop runs designed to steal some of the headlines in connection with the London & North Eastern Railway's (LNER) new scheduled non-stop service from 1 May between London King's Cross and Edinburgh Waverley – the 'Flying Scotsman'. On 27 April the 'Royal Scot' was run as two separate trains, a nine-coach train to Glasgow behind 'Royal Scot', no. 6113 Cameronian, and a six-coach train for Edinburgh hauled by LMS class 4P 4–4–0, no. 1054. These runs, both to schedule, succeeded in achieving a new British distance record for a non-stop train (the Glasgow run of 401.4 miles behind Cameronian), the longest non-stop run by a 4–4–0 in Great Britain (in fact, the longest run ever made by a 4–4–0 in this country), and the first publicised non-stop run to Edinburgh, a distance of 399.7 miles.

The Symington stop made it impossible for the LMS to compete with the LNER's new daily non-stop service, and in the winter, extra stops were made by the Down service at Rugby, Crewe and Carlisle while the Up service called at Carlisle and Crewe. However, the timings remained the same, at 8¼ hours each way. Although the 'Royal Scot' 4–6–0s had become the standard motive power for the train since 1927, it was not until 1932 that the timings of the train were reduced. The new locomotives, augmented by a further twenty built at Derby from 1929, had been a great success but the heavy work being asked of them on the London–Carlisle, Crewe–Perth and Crewe–Glasgow rotas led to weaknesses including high coal consumption, which was traced to the piston rings, axle boxes that caused bad riding qualities and hot boxes. These defects were corrected by Stanier from 1933.

In 1933, a momentous year for the train, the summer timings were reduced to 7 hours 40 minutes. In that year an eight-coach 'Royal Scot' formation, together with 'Royal Scot' class

4–6–0, no.6100 *Royal Scot*, paid a triumphant visit to North America, covering 11,000 miles in little more than six months. Exhibited in eighty cities and towns, the train was inspected by an astonishing three million people, including Hollywood film stars. The locomotive and train clearly made a great impression on the North American people and on arrival at Vancouver the scenes were chaotic, the crowds being so large that extra police had to be drafted in to turn away thousands of disappointed people. It was not the first visit to North America by a British locomotive as LNWR 2–2–2–2 compound, no.2054, had made a visit in 1893, and the GWR's *King George V* was a visitor in 1927. The actual engine that made the voyage in 1933 was, in fact, no. 6152, *The King's Dragoon Guardsman* which changed identities for the trip because it was due for overhaul when Stanier could incorporate new axleboxes, bogie and springing. On its return from America, it retained its new number and name.

In the year of the 'Royal Scot' visit to North America, a new locomotive design was introduced. The 'Princess Royal' Pacifics were the first express locomotive design of the new CME, William A. Stanier (following his arrival from the GWR at Swindon in the previous year), and were intended to handle the heaviest trains (500 tons) unaided over the gradients at Shap and Beattock. The 'Royal Scot' was usually a heavy train, loaded up to fourteen or fifteen coaches especially in summer, but this was within the capabilities of a 'Princess Royal' single-handed. The formation of the train varied during the 1930s with Edinburgh, Aberdeen, Dundee (ceased in 1933) and Stranraer portions at varying times. The first Stanier-designed coaches appeared in the 'Royal Scot' formation of 1933. From the mid-1930s the loadings were such that the sevice ran as two trains at peak times although there is an instance of a nineteen-coach load being handled by a 'Princess Royal' Pacific in 1934 and arriving in Carlisle on time after its non-stop run from Euston.

The winter timetable of 1936 showed the 'Royal Scot' covering the Glasgow–Euston run in 7 hours 25 minutes – the fastest time yet. The same time was being achieved by the Edinburgh–Euston portion of the train which made it as fast as the 'Flying Scotsman' on its journey to Kings Cross.

In 1937 a new design of express locomotive by Stanier (later Sir William) made its appearance. The 'Princess Coronation' was of similar power rating to the 'Princess Royals' and the first batch appeared as streamliners, designed to work the new fast express between London and Glasgow, the 'Coronation Scot', from 5 July 1937. This was the era of high speed in which the LMS seemed to play catch-up but on 29 June 1937 the first of this new class, 'Coronation', set an official British record speed of 114mph on a test run from Euston to Crewe. The return journey took 2 hours, similar to that of the daily schedules in the electric era from the late 1960s. The first five of these new engines were blue with white stripes to match the coaching stock of the new train, but the second batch of streamliners, nos 6225–9, were red with gold lining. They appeared in 1938 and were followed in the same year by the first non-streamlined examples of the class. The 'Princess Royals' were superseded on the 'Royal Scot' as the regular form of motive power.

By 1938 the Down train reached Glasgow in 7 hours, a considerable reduction in time when compared with the times of only 6 years earlier. However, by now it was not the fastest train between the two cities. This accolade had passed to the 'Coronation Scot' which completed the journey in 6½ hours, albeit with a considerably lighter load. With the start of the winter timetable in 1938 restaurant facilities were withdrawn from the Edinburgh portion of the train and those retained in the Glasgow portion were altered to take account of the change. Before the end of the 1939 summer timetable, the train ran for the last time as the 'Royal Scot' in LMS days on 9 September. Once the war had begun trains became much heavier and the facilities such as catering disappeared. By 1940 the 10 a.m. departures had slowed to 8¾ hours for the northbound train and 8 hours 50 minutes for the Up train, despite its being a non-stop service from Carlisle.

After the war ended, restaurant car facilities were restored (though not to the same standards as before the war), and by 1947 the kitchen cars returned to the train. By the time the title 'Royal

Scot' was re-introduced on 16 February 1948, the day after the centenary of the opening of the Caledonian Railway and completion of the WCML, the LMS had ceased to exist. However, the decision to restore the name on that date had been an LMS decision. Shortly after the war had ended the trains missed out the Carlisle stop, but engine crews were changed at Kingmoor on the northbound train and at Carlisle No. 12 box, south of Citadel station, for the same purpose. By the end of 1946 timings had begun to come down, with 8½ hours for the northbound train in the winter timetables of 1946, although the southbound train was allowed 8¼ hours.

In 1950 the 'Royal Scot' became the first passenger service to employ diesel traction, albeit on an irregular basis. The locomotives concerned were the pioneer mainline diesel electrics, nos 10000 and 10001, which were usually employed in harness. The timing of the train was reduced to 8 hours 25 minutes northbound and 8 hours 13 minutes to Euston at the start of the 1950–1 timetable. This included the reinstated Carlisle stop.

In the summer of 1952 the timings were reduced again to 8 hours as the train was composed of new BR coaching stock. However, the winter timetables added a further ten minutes to the northbound run when loads sometimes amounted to sixteen coaches. In 1956 the train, with its coaches in the new maroon livery, reverted to through engine working using Camden Pacifics from the start of the summer timetable. By this time there was no longer an Edinburgh portion and the stop at Symington had been abandoned. In 1957 BR London Midland Region introduced a new Anglo-Scottish service, the 'Caledonian', following the success of the 'Talisman' on the East Coast Main Line, the previous year. It ran to a scheduled time of 6 hours 40 minutes, only ten minutes slower than the pre-war 'Coronation Scot'. What is less well known is that there had been plans to run such a service in 6¼ hours from the summer of 1956 but the plans were abandoned because of fears of disruptions to evening freight services. The 'Caledonian' was a lightweight train of eight coaches. In that year the 'Royal Scot' was running with a substantially heavier load to a much-reduced time of 7¼ hours, not far behind its 1938 timing.

During the 1950s another class of pioneer diesel was used on the 'Royal Scot'. The locomotives were BR diesel electrics with a 1 Co-Co 1 wheel arrangement and were numbered 10201–3. Of these, no. 10203 was fitted with a more powerful engine and was able to work the train single-handed, whereas the other two locomotives were usually used in tandem.

The winter timetable of 1958 witnessed a significant break with the past, namely a move away from the time-honoured departure of 10 a.m. to 9.50 a.m. from Euston with a journey time of 7 hours 55 minutes and stops at Rugby, Crewe and Carlisle. In the following summer the non-stop working was resumed and the journey time was reduced to 7 hours 25 minutes. Sunday services, incidentally, were typically 2 hours longer in duration. Another major change took place with the introduction of the winter timetable of 1959. The 'Royal Scot' and, indeed, the 'Mid-day Scot' were both run on identical timings to the 'Caledonian', with one stop only at Carlisle and a light load of eight coaches. Furthermore, with a new departure time of 9.05 a.m., regular travellers may have been forgiven for thinking that this was a different train. As it happened, despite the reduced timing of 7¼ hours the change did not find favour with travellers and in the following year a stop was added at Preston, with a view to attracting more business. Meanwhile, the Sunday working was undergoing its own changes with, for two consecutive winters, a Glasgow arrival at Buchanan Street (closed later in the 1960s) and five stops en route, adding Beattock and Motherwell to the more usual calling stops at Rugby, Crewe and Carlisle.

In 1959 the London Midland Region received its first batch of main line diesels following the Modernisation Plan, and English Electric Type 4 2000hp diesel electrics appeared on the service later that year, although the 'Princess Coronation' class was still used. Indeed, it was not until 1961 that the Type 4 diesels (later class 40s) completely took over the 'Royal Scot' service. In the summer timetable that year the timing to Glasgow came down to 7 hours with a stop at Carlisle. However, once the electrification programme had begun on the WCML it was inevitable that services would be affected. Initially, the disruption was to the section of line south of Weaver

Junction and in the 1960–1 winter timetable there was a recovery allowance of 48 minutes for northbound trains as far as Preston.

During the early 1960s the departure time from Euston appeared to vary within the range of 9.05 a.m. and 9.50 a.m. every summer and winter timetable (but the Up train was booked to leave Glasgow at the traditional time of 10 a.m.) while journey times fluctuated between 7 hours 5 minutes and 7 hours 20 minutes during this period. The Preston stop only lasted during the winter timetables of 1960–1 and 1961–2 before the train reverted to calling only at Carlisle for much of the next four years (except Sundays). A notable development was the return of the old departure time of 10 a.m. in the winter timetable of 1963 and this continued until the summer of 1965 when it moved away from this time for good.

In 1966 the first stage of the WCML electrification was completed with a full electric service from Euston to Liverpool and Manchester. This had benefits for a large number of services including the 'Royal Scot' which, though increased to thirteen coaches, saw its timing drastically reduced to 2 hours (actually 2 hours 1 minute northbound and 1 hour 59 minutes southbound) to Crewe, where there was a regular stop for a change of traction. The 'Princess Coronation' class had already shown that it was possible to cover the 158 miles to Crewe in less than 2 hours but now these times had become routine – a daily occurrence. Despite the engineering work that the services had to contend with, the overall journey time to Glasgow had fallen to 6 hours 35 minutes. The high speeds by electric traction south of Crewe played a big part in the quicker timings, but north of Crewe there were improvements, too, with the train now in the hands of the more powerful Brush Type 4 2750hp diesel electrics that had replaced the earlier Type 4s. Since 1965 the 'Royal Scot' had settled into a 10.05 a.m. departure time from Euston and this continued until 1973–4.

In late-1967 the first English Electric Type 4 2700hp diesel electrics were introduced and worked the 'Royal Scot' north of Crewe. From 1970–1 they worked the train in pairs with, inevitably, faster times. For instance, the thirteen-coach train was booked to cover the 141 miles between Crewe and Carlisle in 116 minutes. However, electrification work north of Crewe, caused disruptions and in 1971–2 the train acquired a new calling point at Blackburn on Sundays when rerouted along the Settle and Carlisle. After the following year Blackburn was dropped, together with Willesden Junction, which had also enjoyed the patronage of the Sunday train. On the plus side the train received new, quieter Mark 2D coaches with air conditioning. Also, track-work improvements had allowed trains to reach 100mph along sections of the WCML in Scotland by 1972, and in 1973 the new class 87s were introduced. In the 1973–4 timetable the journey time was reduced by as much as forty minutes to 5 hours 59 minutes. At the beginning of that timetable a change of traction was still required and the pairs of what had now become class 50s continued to do sterling work.

However, when electrification to Glasgow was completed, the era of the 'Electric Scots' began in a blaze of publicity. The 'Royal Scot', with a new departure time of 10.45 a.m. that would last into the 1980s, covered the journey in 5 hours, its best time in each direction, with effect from 6 May 1974. Departure time from Glasgow was 10.10 a.m. There was another significant move with the introduction of the new service, namely the dropping of Carlisle from the schedule after decades of association with the train. Instead, Preston became the only stop until the early 1980s when Carlisle reappeared.

Mark 3 BR standard coaches were introduced on the 'Royal Scot' service towards the end of 1975 and on 11 July 1977 a significant milestone was reached when the fiftieth anniversary of the train was commemorated. A class '87' electric, no. 87001, was renamed *Royal Scot* before leaving Euston for Glasgow on that day. The timings were eased in the late 1970s when further track-work maintenance became necessary. These times fluctuated; the slowest schedules were between 1981 and 1983 when the 'Royal Scot' was allowed as much as 5 hours 26 minutes northbound and 5 hours 28 minutes southbound. During the 1980s and 1990s the departure time from Euston was varied between 9.45 a.m. from 1983 and 10.50 a.m. in 1993. Preston and Carlisle remained the regular calling points but Lancaster and, to a lesser extent, Oxenholme appeared on the train's itinerary. Even the famous name was tampered with briefly, the service being described as the 'Royal Scot Limited' in the late 1980s.

In the final BR years the journey time of the 'Royal Scot' was reduced to below 5 hours with a best time of 4 hours 43 minutes in 1990–1. Haulage was by class 87s and 90s but class 86s still handled the express at this time. These were the principal locomotives inherited by Virgin Rail when they began operations in 1997, and they continued until the Pendolino revolution in 2004. The timings had slackened up to that time and in June 2002 the 'Royal Scot' disappeared from the timetables. It reappeared as a footnote in 2004–5 but then vanished again as new, faster schedules were introduced using the Pendolinos, the quickest trains reaching Glasgow in under 4 hours 30 minutes.

2007 marked the eightieth anniversary of the 'Royal Scot', one of the most famous brand names among trains, and yet, at the end of 2006, Virgin West Coast announced that it was transferring the name to Riviera Trains for use on a special charter train. Refurbishment of the 'Royal Scot' coaching set was completed in 2008. It is comforting to know that the 'Royal Scot' title is still considered to be of commercial interest, and it is to be hoped that the train and the engines of the same name have long-term futures.

Two LNWR types are seen hard at work, in true LNWR spirit. A Webb 'Precedent' 2–4–0, no.749, pilots a 'George the Fifth' 4–4–0, no. 228, on an Up express south of Carlisle on 26 June 1920, near to the end of the LNWR era. The 'Precedents' were designed by Webb and achieved fame in the Races to the North of 1895 when one of their class, no. 790 *Hardwicke*, ran between Crewe and Carlisle at an average speed of 67.2mph with, admittedly, a light train. *Hardwicke* was set aside for preservation when it was withdrawn in 1932. The 'George the Fifth' 4–4–0s were one of the more successful designs for the LNWR and were used as pilot engines briefly in the first few months of the 'Royal Scot' service until sufficient numbers of the new 'Royal Scot' class had been built. (*Rail Archive Stephenson Photomatics*)

The famous Caledonian Railway Cardean 4–6–0, no. 903 stands at Glasgow Central, in the company's blue livery, awaiting departure with an Anglo-Scottish express. It will work as far as Carlisle, the southern extent of the Caledonian Railway's territory. These locomotives were used regularly on the 10 am express until the Grouping. No. 907 of the same class was destroyed in the Quintinshill railway disaster of 1915, the worst in Britain in terms of death toll. *(Rail Archive Stephenson Photomatics)*

Bowen-Cooke's 'Claughton' 4–6–0s became the LNWR's principal express locomotive from 1913. These 4–6–0s became the regular motive power on the 10 a.m. Anglo-Scottish expresses and were used initially on the 'Royal Scot' service between Euston and Carnforth until the arrival of the replacement 4–6–0s from the summer of 1927. Once Stanier introduced his new express locomotive designs, the 'Claughtons' were rapidly withdrawn, the last un-rebuilt example being scrapped in 1935. A 'Claughton' 4–6–0, no. 5918, is seen taking water at Bushey troughs on a down relief 'Royal Scot' service in August 1931. *(Rail Archive Stephenson Photomatics)*

The Midland Compound 4–4–0s played their part in the running of WCML express operations. Indeed, they had a regular turn on the newly-named 'Royal Scot' service in 1927, running in pairs between Carnforth and Glasgow until Fowler's 'Royal Scots' emerged later in the same year. Here we see no. 1101 piloting an unidentified 'Silver Jubilee' on a fourteen-coach train tackling Shap on 27 August 1937. Another member of this class, no. 1054, achieved fame on 27 April 1928 when it ran the Edinburgh portion of the non-stop 'Royal Scot' and thus achieved a record for distance running by a British 4–4–0. (*Rail Archive Stephenson Photomatics*)

The introduction of the 'Royal Scot' 4–6–0s from 1927 onwards made a great difference to the LMS motive power department as the heavier trains could be hauled single-handed. This can be seen from the view of no. 6132 Phoenix (later re-named *The King's Regiment Liverpool*) at the head of the fifteen-coach 'Royal Scot' service near Carpenders Park in August 1931. The height of the coal above the top of the tender appears to justify the need for the larger capacity tenders with which they were fitted in the 1930s. The 'Royal Scots' became the first new LMS locomotives to bear names, half of them being assigned the names of British Army regiments and others adopting the names of locomotives from the early days of railways. (*Rail Archive Stephenson Photomatics*)

Following a fatal derailment at Leighton Buzzard caused by drifting smoke from the chimney, the 'Royal Scots' were fitted with smoke deflectors from the early 1930s. These were the first LMS locomotives to carry deflectors but only after various experiments to deflect the smoke, most of which did little to improve the appearance of these engines. This view of no. 6146 *Jenny Lind* was taken in the early 1930s. It was re-named *The Rifle Brigade* in 1935 or 1936. *(J.T. Rutherford, www.transporttreasury.co.uk)*

Following the successful conversion of two 'Jubilees' it was decided to rebuild all of the 'Scots' from 1943, a process that took nearly twelve years. In rebuilt form they continued as front line motive power until the 1960s. Withdrawals began in 1962 and the last survivor was withdrawn at the beginning of 1966. No. 46120 *Royal Inniskilling Fusilier* was rebuilt in 1944 and is paired with one of the larger capacity tenders fitted in the late 1930s. It is seen at Crewe in early BR lined-black livery before the addition of new smoke deflectors. *(M. Robertson, www.transporttreasury.co.uk)*

'Royal Scot' 4-6-0, no.46153 The Royal Dragoon, is in charge of the Up 'Royal Scot' train at Crewe on 2 June 1953, the Coronation day of Queen Elizabeth 11. The locomotive is wearing a special crown headboard that was provided for about two weeks on either side of Coronation day. The 'Royal Scot' was one of four trains to be provided with such a headboard. *(R.J. Leonard/Kidderminster Railway Museum)*

The 'Royal Scot' in its final form is seen to good effect in this pleasing study at Carlisle Kingmoor depot. The engine is no. 46166 *London Rifle Brigade* seen here on 30 August 1964, two months before it was withdrawn from service. The diagonal stripe on the cab-side indicates that it was banned from working under the 25KV overhead wires because of height restrictions. All the remaining survivors of the 'Royal Scots', 'Patriots' and 'Clans' were based here in the mid-1960s. In the 1960s this depot grew in importance while Upperby shed declined, prior to its closure in 1966. Kingmoor survived until January 1968, months before the elimination of steam in August of that year. Two engines of this class are preserved including no. 46100 *Royal Scot* and no. 46115 *Scots Guardsman*, both of which have been restored to working order. *(Hugh Ballantyne)*

By 1933 the 'Royal Scot' was hauled by a 'Pacific' for the first time, following the introduction of the 'Princess Royal' class in the same year. There remained a need for a locomotive that could handle the heaviest loads up Shap and Beattock unaided. The 'Princess Royal' answered that requirement and was William A. Stanier's first express locomotive design. To many it bore a resemblance to the GWR 'King' class (Stanier moved from Swindon to join the LMS) but in this view of no. 6200 *The Princess Royal* passing Newton, on the outskirts of Glasgow, with the Up 'Royal Scot', the similarities appear to be more in the detail than in the general appearance. The date is 31 March 1934 and the time 10.16 a.m. Note the small Midland tender behind the engine. *(Rail Archive Stephenson Photomatics)*

Initial teething problems with the first two 'Princess Royal' Pacifics led to a successful redesign of the boilers. Apart from their feats of haulage, these locomotives demonstrated the feasibility of sustained high-speed running when in 1936 no. 6201 *Princess Elizabeth* ran in both directions to a special schedule of 6 hours and comfortably ran within the schedule. The return journey from Glasgow was reduced to 5 hours 44 minutes, an average of 70 mph, comparable with speeds in the electric era. In the 1930s the 'Princess Royal' 4–6–2s received larger capacity tenders as shown with no. 46205 *Princess Victoria*, in green livery. The locomotive is seen at Camden in between duties. The 'Princess Royal' class was one of the most powerful of all British locomotive designs. They were withdrawn in 1961 and 1962. There are two survivors in preservation, namely, no. 46201 *Princess Elizabeth* and no. 46203 *Princess Margaret Rose*. (*W. Hermiston, www.transporttreasury.co.uk*)

Described as Stanier's masterpiece, the first five of the 'Princess Coronation' Pacifics appeared in 1937 in streamlined form. The livery was blue with white stripes, matched by the train, the 'Coronation Scot', a new high-speed service introduced in the same year. In 1937 no. 6223 *Princess Alice* was seen leaving Euston at the head of the 'Coronation Scot', scheduled to cover the 401 miles to Glasgow in 6½ hours. Judging by the pristine condition of the buffers and the interest on the platform, the locomotive is probably newly built. These locomotives were paired with tenders that could hold up to 10 tons of coal and were fitted with steam-operated coal pushers making the job of the fireman that much easier. No. 6223 was converted to its non-streamlined form in 1946 and by 1949 all the other members of the class had been similarly treated. *(Rail Archive Stephenson Photomatics)*

After five more streamliners were completed in 1938, the next five in the series emerged from Crewe Works in non-streamlined form. No. 6234 *Duchess of Abercorn* is seen in original condition at Crewe North on 14 August 1938. Shortly after this picture was taken it was involved in trials with exceptionally heavy loads over Shap and Beattock to test its capabilities. As a result of its performances it was fitted with a double chimney and a double blastpipe before being put to test again with astonishing results. One of the most memorable feats was its ability to haul a twenty-coach load up Beattock at a speed no lower than 62mph. It also achieved a drawbar horsepower of 2511, the highest recorded by a steam locomotive in Britain. (*www.transporttreasury.co.uk*)

There are not a lot of photographs of the non-streamlined 'Princess Coronation' locomotives in original condition as only five appeared before the war. Then restrictions were placed on the photography of railway premises, and all but one was fitted with smoke deflectors by 1947. This pre-war shot at Camden shows no. 6233 *Duchess of Sutherland* heading north with the Down 'Royal Scot' in September 1938. The engine was two months old at the time. (*The late Eric Woods, Peter Fitton Collection*)

The 'Princess Coronation' Pacifics took on a distinctly improved appearance when fitted with smoke deflectors as seen at Crewe North with no. 46234 *Duchess of Abercorn* with double chimney and in black livery in July 1949. Smoke deflectors were fitted from 1945 and, with double chimneys and double blastpipes, they remained in this form to the end of their lives. *(W. Hermiston, www.transporttreasury.co.uk)*

Although the 'Royal Scot' name was conferred in 1927, it was not until 1950 that a headboard was provided for the locomotive in charge of the train. In steam days there were two main styles, each with variants. The first style was the rectangular board with semi-circular ends as worn by 'Princess Coronation' no. 46257 *City of Salford*, seen passing Watford Junction with the 'Royal Scot'. This engine, the last of its class, was the only one to be built after nationalisation in 1948. *(J. Robertson, www.transporttreasury.co.uk)*

The other main style of headboard was introduced in the early 1950s and was of the familiar arched variety. Again there were different versions of this headboard and the name included the definite article so that in the case of 'Princess Coronation' no. 46246 *City of Manchester*, ready to leave Glasgow Central on 21 July 1959, the headboard read 'The Royal Scot'. In 1960 this engine, in red livery, was the last member of the class to have its sloping smokebox removed. Three of this class survive today in preservation. They are no. 46229 *Duchess of Hamilton*, no. 46233 *Duchess of Sutherland* and no. 46235 *City of Birmingham*. (*Gavin Morrison*)

While the 'Princess Coronation' 4–6–2s remained the principal motive power for trains such as the 'Royal Scot' until the dawn of the 1960s, this train was the first to employ diesel power. The first of two 1600hp diesel electric locomotives with a Co-Co wheel arrangement, no. 10000, was introduced by the LMS in 1947, while no. 10001 was built in BR ownership. They came about as the result of a visit by LMS officials to America. From early in the BR era these locomotives were often seen as a pair on the 'Royal Scot' service. On 13 August 1950 they are seen heading away from Crewe on the southbound service. The headboard worn by no. 10000 is the earliest of the moveable headboards, having been introduced on 5 June 1950. (*J.D. Darby*)

A further three pioneer main line diesels comprising 10201–3 were built at Ashford works for the BR Southern Region. Unlike the American influence on nos 10000 and 10001, the new diesels appeared to borrow more from European designs. They moved to the London Midland Region in the mid-1950s and in 1957 nos 10201 and 10202 (1600hp each unit) were tried out in tandem on the 'Royal Scot'. Then no. 10203 (20000hp) operated as a single unit on the train and became a regular performer on the service in 1957 and 1958. While it is purely conjecture, no. 10203, may have been used with a view to gauging the likely performance of the English Electric Type 4s that were being built that year and which had a similar power rating, weight and wheel arrangement. No. 10203 is seen climbing Madeley Bank, south of Crewe, with the Up 'Royal Scot' on 20 July 1958. All the pioneer diesel electric locomotives were withdrawn in 1963. *(John Hilton)*

It is believed that one of the new 2000hp English Electric Type 4s (later Class 40s) made its first appearance on the 'Royal Scot' in September 1959 but it was not until 1961 when they became the principal motive power on this train. However, 'Princess Coronation' Pacifics were still to be seen in charge until the last year of their working lives. At Carlisle, 'Princess Coronation', no. 46230 *Duchess of Buccleuch* has just brought in the 'Royal Scot' from Glasgow and is coming off the train while English Electric Type 4, no. D326 (which, two months earlier, had been the locomotive involved in the Great Train Robbery) waits in a centre road to take the train on to London on 27 October 1963. The *Duchess of Buccleuch* was withdrawn from service in the following month. *(T. Noble, David Chatfield Collection)*

An English Electric Type 4, no. D327, is at Harthope on the latter stages of the climb to Beattock summit with an unusually light load for the 'Royal Scot' of eight coaches. This was as a result of a decision by the authorities to run lighter loads on the 'Royal Scot' and the 'Mid-day Scot' but to reduced timings, similar to that of the 'Caledonian'. The decision was not a success and eventually led to heavier trains once again. The Glasgow-bound train is seen on Saturday 20 May 1961. *(Gavin Morrison)*

From 1966 the Brush Type 4s (later 47s) took over haulage of the 'Royal Scot' for what turned out to be a relatively short period. They were introduced in 1962 on the Eastern Region but they were surprisingly late in arriving on the WCML at which point they became the regular motive power for most Anglo-Scottish expresses. As far as the 'Royal Scot' was concerned, the work of these locomotives was confined mainly to the section north of Crewe once electrification had reached Euston. Towards the end of 1967 new English Electric Type 4s (Class 50s) were introduced to the London Midland Region and by 1968 they had replaced the Brush Type 4s on this service. On 18 October 1967 no. D1620 is emerging from the Lune Gorge with a southbound express. *(Tom Heavyside)*

Carnforth no. 2 signal-box witnesses the passage of an unusual pairing of locomotives on the northbound 'Royal Scot' on 28 July 1967. In fact, the train engine, Brush Type 4 no.D1621 (later no. 47766), made an unscheduled stop for assistance and having acquired a helping hand in the form of Brush Type 2 no. D7638 (later no. 25288), the whole ensemble including fifteen coaches snakes out of the Down loop and through Carnforth to resume its journey north. *(Peter Fitton)*

The first of the WCML electric locomotives appeared in 1959–60 and ran most passenger services on the expanding electrified routes south of Manchester and Liverpool. In 1966, when electrification was completed to London, a new class was introduced, the AL6 (later 86), and they helped to bring the London–Crewe schedule down to a routine 2 hours. This had its effect on Anglo-Scottish services too. The 86s continued to be used on trains such as the 'Royal Scot' until the end of locomotive haulage. At Glasgow Central, no. 86042 is seen leaving with the 17.45 'Midland Scot' for Birmingham on 23 May 1974, shortly after the new electric timetables had been introduced throughout. *(Tom Heavyside)*

In 1967 the first of a new series of English Electric Co-Co diesels appeared on the WCML. The prototype of these engines was known as DP2, which emerged from Vulcan Works in 1962. Bodily, DP2 bore a close resemblance to the Deltics and was the last in a line of diesel locomotives that borrowed from American designs. DP2 was written off after an accident at Thirsk in 1967 but, in the following year, the 2700hp production models, with flat-fronted cabs, were at work on the 'Royal Scot' north of Crewe and performed admirably in a stop-gap role prior to electrification through to Glasgow. On Saturday 7 March 1970 no. D405 is seen in charge of the Down 'Royal Scot' at Shap Summit. In 1970/1 these engines were used in pairs on all the heavier trains with a consequent improvement in timings that had come down to below 6 hours by the summer of 1973. (*Gavin Morrison*)

In 1973 the Class 87 was introduced. The most powerful locomotive to date at 5000hp, they were designed for intensive working on both passenger and freight along the WCML. It became the usual motive power on the 'Royal Scot' and no. 87018 is seen crossing the River Clyde and entering Glasgow Central with this service, composed of Mark III coaches on 6 March 1976. *(Tom Heavyside)*

In the 1990s the Class 87s shared their duties on the 'Royal Scot' with both Class 86s and the newer Class 90s until the end of locomotive haulage at the dawn of a new century. An unidentified Class 90 is seen on the northbound service near Garstang on 17 March 1990. The Lancaster Canal is in the foreground. *(Tom Heavyside)*

London to the Chilterns

Euston station is the principal starting point for rail travellers between London and Glasgow. However the Euston of the steam and of the electric eras are quite different from each other. In the days of steam the intending passenger's first view of Euston station was of the huge Doric arch, arguably the most imposing entrance of any British station. In 1962 this familiar landmark, along with much of the old Euston station, was demolished to make way for a new gateway to Scotland, in keeping with the dawn of the Electric Age. The modern Euston of glass, white mosaic facings and black granite columns, expansive concourse with direct links to the underground system was completed in 1968.

Leaving Euston, the climb towards Camden, up the once formidable bank, represented a challenging start to the journey, and rear end assistance was often required. At Camden one of the principal locomotive depots was situated on the left. It was home to many of the principal express locomotive types on this line until its closure in 1961. Almost opposite the site of the shed is the Chalk Farm Roundhouse, once a locomotive depot itself, but more recently used as an art centre. Originally known as the Camden Town Engine House when built for the London & Birmingham Railway, it was replaced by Camden depot in 1871. The former North London Railway tracks join from the right.

Beyond Primrose Hill Tunnels, the first two stations out of Euston are encountered on the right-hand side. They are South Hampstead and Kilburn High Road, used by local trains only. About half way between these stations the line passes under Abbey Road, home of the EMI recording studios and made famous by the Beatles' album cover of the same name. The latter station takes its name from Kilburn High Road that crosses the line at the far end of the station. It is, in fact, the A5 trunk road to Holyhead, and is encountered several times during the earlier part of the journey. Local stations at Queen's Park and Kensal Green precede Kensal Green Tunnel and, up on the left beyond the tunnels, is the boundary to Kensal Green cemetery, which contains the tombs of, among others, Isambard Kingdom Brunel and the writer William Makepeace Thackeray.

Under Scrubs Lane, which leads to Wormwood Scrubs prison, the train passes Willesden Junction. Look out for the branch from Clapham Junction joining the main line on the left, while the former North London Railway crosses over at Willesden Junction High Level. Willesden motive power depot once stood on the left, while further back and out of sight lay the principal Great Western Railway steam depot at Old Oak Common, a reminder that at this point the West Coast Main Line and the former GWR main line out of Paddington are at their closest point to each other being a mere half mile apart. Beyond the bridge, carrying the former Midland Railway line between Acton and Cricklewood, the local trains diverge away from the main line to call at Harlesden and Stonebridge Park stations. The main line crosses over the North Circular Road and the local lines (including the Bakerloo underground line), which are now on the left, before passing through Wembley Central station. The Wembley stadium of 2007 is visible on the right, having replaced its predecessor that was built for the British Empire Exhibition of 1924.

A few hundred yards before Wembley Central the train passes under the former Great Central Railway (GCR) main line from Marylebone to Sheffield and Manchester. Although it was the last main line to be built in England it was reduced in 1966 to little more than a secondary route of local importance, serving Princes Risborough and Banbury. Beyond North Wembley and South Kenton stations a brief view can be had of Harrow on the Hill on the left with the tower and spire of St Mary's parish church. Harrow hill itself is a large mass of London clay rising to over 400ft above sea level and one of the highest points in Greater London. The whole of this area forms part of the Thames Basin, composed of gravels, sands and clays deposited when a shallow sea occupied the basin.

The line is crossed at about 10 miles out by a second former GCR branch to Aylesbury that is also used by the Metropolitan Line trains. Beyond is Kenton station and then, after another mile, Harrow and Wealdstone, the scene of a major railway disaster in 1952 when a Perth–Euston sleeping car express ran into the rear of a local train. The wreckage was struck almost immediately at high speed by a Liverpool express. 112 lives were lost, the second highest death toll for a railway accident in Britain.

Headstone Lane and Hatch End suburban stations follow in quick succession before Greater London is left behind and Hertfordshire is entered. A cutting takes us to Carpenders Park and between this station and Bushey we pass the site of the first set of water troughs along the route. At the final stage of steam locomotive development, the principal LMS locomotives carried tenders with 4,000 gallons of water. As an express locomotive was capable of consuming 3,000 gallons of water for every 100 miles of track covered, it is easy to appreciate why there was a need for water troughs, especially as many of the top expresses covered distances far greater than 100 miles without a stop.

At Bushey station the branch line to the left is for local services to Watford and, a mile further on, Watford town can be seen on the left as the train crosses the River Colne on a viaduct. The parish church of St Mary in Watford High Street is visible with its stout tower and raised stair turret. It is faced in flint, a material that is used on many churches in this part of the country. Approaching Watford Junction, the branch from the Watford High Street joins on the left, while behind the station on the right is the branch line to St Albans. In the fork between the WCML and the branch line is the site of the town's former locomotive depot. Shortly, the train enters a cutting leading to Watford Tunnel leaving Metroland behind.

It is nearly 10 a.m. and 'Princess Coronation' no. 46244 *King George VI* will soon depart London Euston with the 'Royal Scot' express for Glasgow Central on 4 October 1953. The headboard has a Hunting Stewart tartan background. This locomotive set what is believed to be a record time for steam between Crewe and Euston when in charge of the 'Caledonian' express in 1957. It passed through Crewe and, from there, proceeded to reel off the 158 miles to Euston in 118 minutes, a minute faster and with a marginally heavier load than the famous publicity run by Coronation in 1937, although the earlier run was made from a standing start. *(R. Butterfield/Initial Photographics)*

At the head of 'The Merseyside Express' alongside platform 1 on 19 May 1958 is 'Princess Royal' no. 46207 *Princess Arthur of Connaught*, whose shed code 8A indicates that the locomotive was based at Liverpool's largest depot, Edge Hill. The train was a non-stop express covering the 193½ miles between Liverpool and London in 3 hours 35 minutes. *(J. Robertson, www.transporttreasury.co.uk)*

Unofficially, the oldest named train, 'The Irish Mail' is an early morning arrival at Euston from Holyhead behind Crewe-based 'Princess Royal' no. 46200 *The Princess Royal*. *(Derek Potton, www.transporttreasury.co.uk)*

A distinguished locomotive stands at the head of 'The Ulster Express', an early evening departure on 28 September 1954 from Euston for Heysham, providing a connection with the boat service to Belfast. The locomotive is 'Royal Scot' no. 46100 *Royal Scot* and was based locally at Camden depot, denoted by the code 1B. This engine started life as no. 6152 but changed identities with the original no. 6100 as it was in better condition to endure the rigours of an extensive and successful tour of the USA and Canada in 1933. On returning to the UK, the locomotive kept its new identity and, although it was one of the first of its class to be withdrawn from service, it was subsequently rescued for preservation. *(A.G. Ellis, www.transporttreasury.co.uk)*

A 'Silver Jubilee' 4–6–0, no. 45556 *Nova Scotia* stands at the head of an express after arrival at Euston's platform 1. The attractive curve of the old fishbone roof at Euston is shown to good effect in this picture of 17 September 1959. *(D. Chatfield)*

For all the stately arrivals and imposing departures there were the workaday activities that went largely unnoticed by the public. Every time a steam train arrived, the coaches would have to be removed to the sidings in order to release the locomotive at the buffers. Here we see Stanier 2–6–4 tank, no. 42478, at the head of empty stock at platform 1 on 7 May 1952, destined for the carriage sheds nearby or further out. The shed code, 1A, at the front end of this locomotive shows that it is based at London's motive power depot at Willesden. (*E.S. Murrell courtesy of the Stephenson Locomotive Society*)

Immediately on leaving Euston station there is a steep climb up Camden Bank followed by a more gradual climb, with brief respites, as far as Tring in the Chilterns. Passing Camden shed to the right of the picture, 'Patriot', no. 45537 *Private E. Sykes, V.C.*, struggles with a heavy Blackpool train on a damp day in October 1949. In the distance the track can be seen dipping down towards Euston. (*R.F. Roberts courtesy of the Stephenson Locomotive Society*)

The 'Royal Scot' is seen in the light and shade of Camden's cuttings, less than a mile out of Euston, with 'Princess Coronation' no. 46254 *City of Stoke-on-Trent* at the head in August 1959. At a lower level, beyond the locomotive, is a Northampton train. (*A.E. Durrant, www.transporttreasury.co.uk*)

The first station out of Euston at the time this picture was taken was South Hampstead, used by local services only. Here is BR 2–6–0 Class 2, no. 78043, with empty coaching stock from Euston on 31 May 1963. This class of locomotives, based at Willesden depot, was the last to be seen on a regular basis at Euston where they were used on pilot duties until 1965. The train is passing under the bridge carrying the former Great Central main line from Marylebone station to Leicester, Nottingham and Sheffield. (*R.F. Roberts courtesy of the Stephenson Locomotive Society*)

Fowler 2–6–4 tank engines were used on suburban services as well as empty coaching stock duties. No. 42367 is seen passing Kilburn High Road in 1961. *(A.E. Durrant, www.transporttreasury.co.uk)*

A stranger is seen at Willesden Junction station in the form of ex-Southern Railway 4–6–0 'Lord Nelson', no. 30851 *Sir Francis Drake*. Although it was rare to see one of the top link locomotives from any other region at Willesden, it was not unusual to see a former Southern Railway locomotive in this area working on an inter-regional freight from south London. It is said that the 'Lord Nelsons' played some part in the ultimate design of the LMS 'Royal Scots'. *(Rex Conway)*

Just around the corner from the West Coast Main Line at Willesden stood the large depot bearing the code 1A. It housed freight engines and all-purpose types, although even the largest classes were based here briefly in the early 1960s when diesels took over their duties on front-line expresses. By 17 January 1965, when this picture was taken, much of the stock consisted of freight and general purpose locos with, in the left foreground, two Stanier 8F 2–8–0s, nos 48624 and 48387, two Stanier Class 5 4–6–0s, nos 45001 and 44771, side by side, and on the right, two Fowler 0–6–0 tanks (known as 'Jintys'), nos 47435 and, behind it, 47432. *(Hugh Ballantyne)*

Wembley Central station plays host to a local electric service on the right as LMS Compound 4–4–0 no. 41122 passes by with the 7.20 a.m. Euston–Rugby on 25 May 1958. At the time this was a regular summer timetable duty for Rugby-based Compounds but no. 41122 was withdrawn at the end of the year. Until the advent of the 'Royal Scots' these locomotives were used in pairs on the 'Royal Scot' service and its predecessor between Carnforth and Glasgow. Sister engine, no. 1054, achieved fame by running the six-coach Edinburgh portion of the 'Royal Scot' non-stop from Euston on 27 April 1928 as a publicity coup prior to the LNER's new non-stop London–Edinburgh daily service, the 'Flying Scotsman'. *(Alec Swain, www.transporttreasury.co.uk)*

About 10 miles from Euston, Stanier 'Jubilee' 4–6–0, no. 45709 *Implacable*, approaches South Kenton with a Wolverhampton–Euston express on 11 August 1956. Above the rear of the train is the bridge carrying GCR and Metropolitan lines. *(RAS Marketing)*

The 'Royal Scot' is now in the outer suburbs of London with 'Princess Coronation', no. 46254 *City of Stoke-on-Trent* near Harrow and Wealdstone on 24 May 1955. *(www.transporttreasury.co.uk)*

A 'Princess Royal' no. 46209 *Princess Beatrice* makes workmanlike progress with a Euston–Morecambe and Whitehaven express on 19 August 1961 as it leaves Headstone Lane station behind. *(Peter Fitton)*

The first water troughs out of Euston were at Bushey and it appears as if the crew of 'Princess Coronation', no. 46239 *City of Chester*, are making use of the facility on 10 March 1956 as they forge ahead with 'The Ulster Express'. This train ran from Euston to Fleetwood until 1928 when the service was transferred to Heysham. *(www.transporttreasury.co.uk)*

Watford Junction, 18 miles from Euston, is one of the northern outposts of the tube trains, one of which can be seen on the right as 'Princess Coronation', no. 46239 *City of Chester* passes by with an express. *(Derek Potton, www.transporttreasury.co.uk)*

At last the London suburbs are left behind and the train passes through Watford Tunnel and on into the Chiltern Hills. Making its way in the other direction to the capital is 'Royal Scot', no. 46110 *Grenadier Guardsman*, at the head of 'The Shamrock', a Liverpool express due to arrive at Euston at midday on 29 May 1954. The engine's shed code is 8A, confirming its status as an Edge Hill locomotive. *(Stan Creer, www.transporttreasury.co.uk)*

The Chilterns to Rugby

Emerging from the north end of Watford tunnel the train continues along a rising gradient towards the Chiltern Hills; chalk hills with shallow, well-drained soils. Flint is also to be found with the chalk and is seen in local churches. Passing under the M25 motorway and through King's Langley station, look out for the Ovaltine factory on the left which has become a familiar landmark for railway travellers. The River Gade and the Grand Union Canal cross from left to right under the WCML, before we reach Apsley station, which lies on the periphery of the town of Hemel Hempstead to our right. It was designated a new town in 1947 and earmarked to counteract the problems caused by London's growth.

Berkhamsted is 3 miles further on and a familiar sight on the right, immediately before the railway station, is the castle of Berkhamsted, of which stretches of the flint wall can be seen. The castle is understood to date back to the eleventh century and was a favourite residence of Elizabeth I. Chaucer also lived in the castle for a time.

Since entering the Chilterns the railway has followed the course of the river valleys, but beyond Berkhamsted, the contractors who built the London and Birmingham Railway were forced to create substantial engineering works to counteract the rising ground. The results were Northchurch tunnel and, beyond Tring station, one of the most notable engineering works along the whole route, namely Tring cutting. It took four years to complete and was regarded as one of the great feats of the Railway Age. Robert Stephenson was in charge of the works and much of the chalk extracted was used for the embankment to the north of the cutting.

From the chalk uplands of the Chilterns in Hertfordshire, the train continues into Buckinghamshire along a falling gradient to the Vale of Aylesbury with its well-watered clay soil supporting dairy and beef farming. On the right, beyond the cutting, is Beacon Hill, at 756ft, one of several beacon points established during the reign of Elizabeth I to summon men in case of invasion from Spain. The Grand Union Canal is crossed again, this time on the approach to Cheddington station, a former junction for a branch line to Aylesbury. However, the line which ran south-west from the station was dismantled many years ago.

The journey takes us into Bedfordshire, but only briefly. Just long enough, in fact, to take in Leighton Buzzard and Linslade on our right. These towns became known as Leighton Linslade in 1966 although they are separated by the River Ouzel and the Grand Union Canal. Two churches appear on the right as the station is approached. The further of the two is All Saints' Church, about a half mile away, with its Early English steeple rising to 191ft. It is built of ironstone, indicating a change in the source of building materials used. The building dates from the thirteenth century. The area is known for its sand quarries, used in manufacturing and construction processes in this country and abroad.

Beyond Linslade Tunnel we pass back into Buckinghamshire. A series of embankments and cuttings lead to the boundary of Milton Keynes, one of the most significant areas of recent growth. Bletchley is associated with brick-making, an industry that uses materials such as gault clay and sand that are available locally. On the left, just south of Bletchley station, is the line from Oxford and Bicester that once supported a passenger service between Oxford and Cambridge. The line crosses over the WCML via a flyover. North of Bletchley station is the site of the motive power depot on the left which once housed a large allocation of LNWR 0–8–0s. The old and new A5 trunk roads are crossed over a mile beyond Bletchley station. The older, straight formation followed the course of one of the best known of Roman roads, Watling Street, while the modern dual carriageway equivalent is crossed shortly afterwards. The A5 then draws alongside the line on the left as the train takes us past modern industrial sites towards the centre of Milton Keynes on the right, served by a substantial station which was opened in 1982 and is approximately 50 miles from London.

At the north end of Milton Keynes is the town of Wolverton which grew out of the establishment of a large railway works in 1838 and which still constructs and repairs railway coaches today. The extensive works can be seen on the left. On the right the Grand Union Canal can be seen approaching the line and crossing from right to left, under the tracks. Next to the canal on the right is the track-bed of the former branch line to Newport Pagnell. Wolverton station lies to the north end of the town and, as the sidings of the carriage works meet the main line, we cross over the River Great Ouse, which at 156 miles in length is the fourth longest river in England. Beyond the river the train proceeds along a substantial embankment and then through a series of cuttings where lies the site of Castlethorpe station and its former water troughs. Through a gap in the cuttings look out on the right for the splendid tower and spire of St James's Church, Hanslope less than 2 miles away. It is in the Perpendicular style of architecture and has been described as having the finest steeple in Buckinghamshire. It is close to the border with Northamptonshire which is about 2 miles beyond Hanslope.

The site of Roade station, 60 miles from London, lay immediately before the long cutting of the same name. Like Castlethorpe station it closed in 1964. The line splits towards the far end of the substantial cutting and the route to Northampton drops height and veers away to the right. The WCML has become a two-track line for the first time since leaving London. Beyond the cutting the train passes the village of Blisworth whose junction station, with branches to Northampton, Banbury and Stratford-upon-Avon, closed in 1960.

For the next ten miles the Grand Union Canal meanders to the right of the line. Beyond the next tunnel at Stowe Hill, the railway runs onto an embankment, passing Weedon Bec, whose church on the right, St Peter's, boasts a Norman tower. Just beyond the church and canal is the River Nene, one of the principal rivers of the Midlands, but not far from its source at this point. Beyond the cuttings, about 2 miles distant on the left, is Borough Hill by the side of Daventry. On top of the hill are the masts of a broadcasting station. During the Civil War the Royalist Army camped around the hill before their defeat at the decisive Battle of Naseby in 1645.

The M1 draws up alongside the railway while the canal, locked in between the competing modes of transport, climbs through a series of locks and crosses under the line beyond the marina at Whilton locks. As the railway and motorway diverge at the Watford Gap service station, the Grand Union Canal crosses from left to right for the last time before climbing into the Northamptonshire hills. At this point is the site of Welton station, closed in 1958, like that at Weedon. Indeed, the 30-mile stretch of line between Wolverton and Rugby is one of the longest without a station on the WCML.

Shortly, the railway enters a cutting that leads to Kilsby Tunnel, the longest on the WCML at 2,400yds, just under 1½ miles. This caused the greatest engineering problems when the original contractors had to deal with a large band of quicksand. Using pumping engines to remove the water it took eight months to overcome the problem and during that time 1,800 gallons of water were raised every minute and transferred to safe channels of escape. Emerging from the north end of the tunnel we enter the Midlands plain and into the county of Warwickshire. The line from Northampton approaches on the right as the Oxford Canal is crossed, approximately 80 miles from London. The radio transmitting station on the right is at Hillmorton and at 820ft was, at one time, the tallest structure in Britain.

A girder bridge carrying the Great Central Railway main line from Marylebone to Sheffield was once a familiar sight on the approach to Rugby but it was demolished at the end of 2006, forty years after the closure of the GCR main line. There was also a famous locomotive testing station on the right but that too has gone. It was built as late as 1948 and one of only six such plants in the world for testing the performance of steam locomotives. The former locomotive depot lay to the right of the station. Rugby is known for the manufacture of cement and for its engineering works, but little is visible from the line today.

A pre-war scene at Berkhamsted shows LNWR signal, signal-box and traditional roof skirting. LMS 'Royal Scot', no. 6161 *King's Own* sweeps round the curve with the 9.40 a.m. Llandudno–Euston on 19 August 1939, just days before the outbreak of war. (*H.C. Casserley*)

A rebuilt 'Patriot', no. 45521 *Rhyl* makes progress through the Chilterns with an express in 1952. A striking feature of this scene is how neat the track and banks appear. *(F. & R. Hewitt courtesy of the Stephenson Locomotive Society)*

This relatively modern view of Tring Cutting can only give some idea of the enormity of the project to carve out a railway from the chalk with men and picks; no labour-saving machinery here when this task was in hand in the 1830s. The cutting is about 2 miles in length and the section seen here, with some of the chalk visible, represents no more than a half mile. Looking down on the train, a Euston-bound express hauled by Class 86 no. 86016 on 16 July 1977, one sees a major engineering work that has changed little with the passage of time. Not even the gantries for the electric wires appear obtrusive. *(Tom Heavyside)*

Tring station sees the 'Royal Scot' on its way to London, hauled by 'Princess Royal' no. 46201 *Princess Elizabeth* on 9 August 1957. This class of thirteen locomotives was built from 1933 to handle the heaviest Anglo-Scottish expresses including the 'Royal Scot'. From 1938 however, when the 'Princess Coronation' class was introduced, they were used infrequently on the train. Instead, they were seen on other Anglo-Scottish services such as the 'Mid-Day Scot' and Birmingham–Glasgow trains as well as the principal Liverpool expresses. No. 46201 actually holds the record for the fastest runs by steam between London and Glasgow when on test in 1936. Happily, it can still be seen today in preservation. *(J. Robertson, www.transporttreasury.co.uk)*

Cheddington was a junction station with a branch line for Aylesbury operated at one time by old LNWR 2–4–2 tanks, such as Bletchley-based no. 46601 in the bay platform on 21 August 1950. The last of this class was withdrawn in 1955. The main line lies to the left below the footbridge. *(R.F. Roberts courtesy of the Stephenson Locomotive Society)*

It is 12.05 p.m. and 'Royal Scot', no. 46169 *The Boy Scout*, is 50 minutes into its journey as it emerges from the north end of the castellated Linslade Tunnel with the northbound 'Welshman' on 7 July 1962. The train ran between London and Llandudno with through coaches to Pwllheli and Portmadoc. *(Peter Fitton)*

An unrebuilt 'Patriot' no. 45513, one of the handful of unnamed members of this class, waits at Bletchley station with an Up stopping train in August 1957. The locomotive was a Carlisle Upperby engine and so was probably between longer distance duties at the time. *(RAS Marketing)*

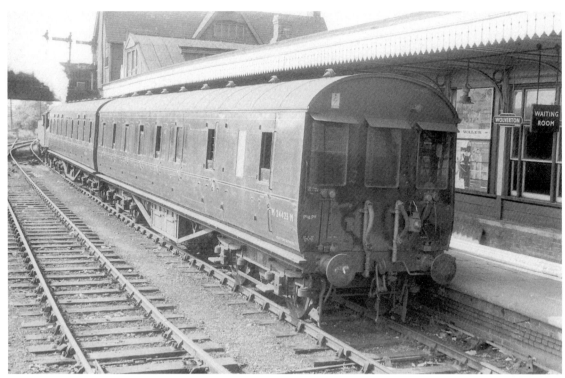

At various places along the West Coast Main Line it was possible to see push-pull services operated by a tank engine with usually two or three coaches. The motor coach would be connected to the engine's controls enabling the driver to control the train from the opposite end to the tank engine. This saved the engine from running around its coaches, a useful saving when the journey was short such as that between Wolverton and Newport Pagnell. In this picture of Wolverton's branch platform, the motor coach is prominent with Ivatt Class 2 2–6–2 tank, no. 41222, at the far end on 7 July 1962. This was to become the last push-pull service on the London Midland Region and was withdrawn on 7 September 1964. *(Peter Fitton)*

A 'Princess Royal' no. 46208 *Princess Helena Victoria* is seen taking water while on the Up fast line at Castlethorpe Troughs in charge of the 10 a.m. Liverpool–Euston service on 23 June 1962. The loco is running with the boiler of former sister engine, no. 46202, that was withdrawn from service following the major rail crash at Harrow and Wealdstone in 1952. *(Peter Fitton)*

In the depths of Roade cutting, the lines to Northampton veer away and the West Coast Main Line becomes a two-track railway for the first time. In this picture we see a 'Royal Scot', no. 46143 *The South Staffordshire Regiment*, at the head of a Euston–Manchester express overtaking a stopping train on 12 May 1951. The locomotive is in rebuilt condition but without smoke plates and is a member of the class that has been timed at 100mph, the occasion being another London–Manchester service, but on the Midland line out of St Pancras with the 'Palatine' in 1960. *(R.F. Roberts courtesy of the Stephenson Locomotive Society)*

Blisworth station was a junction for Northampton and Peterborough to the east and Towcester, Stratford-upon-Avon and Banbury to the west. The western connection was along the Stratford-upon-Avon & Midland Junction Railway, a company that made a habit of connecting up to the north-south main lines including the Midland line at Broom, the Great Western at Fenny Compton, the Great Central at Woodford Junction and the Midland again, at Ravenstone Wood Junction. 'Princess Coronation' no. 46241 *City of Edinburgh* approaches Blisworth from the south with the Down 'Mid-Day Scot' on 14 May 1951. The bay platforms for the east and west lie on the other sides of the main platforms. Note the old wooden wagons in the sidings, the water column at the end of the main-line platform and the bracket signals apparently suspended in mid air by the smoke and steam from the locomotive. *(M.N. Bland, www.transporttreasury.co.uk)*

Since the building of the M1, the section of track near Welton has become noted for the rivalry between train and road vehicles. Nowadays there is no contest as the Pendolinos hurtle past at speeds well in excess of 100mph but in the days of steam the rivalry was more evenly pitched. Here, 'Royal Scot' no. 46170 *British Legion* passes a quiet motorway with an assortment of coaches and wagons on their way north on 6 June 1962. This locomotive was the first 'Royal Scot' to be rebuilt, having started life as the experimental high-pressure version of the 'Royal Scots' known as no. 6399 *Fury. (Peter Fitton)*

A Stanier Class 8F, no. 48263, passes the remains of Welton station on 6 June 1962 with a mineral train heading north. Although the station closed in 1958 there were still the remnants of Welton including platform, sidings and loading bay, all to be swept away from wayside stations in the 1960s and 1970s. *(Peter Fitton)*

A little further on from Welton is Kilsby Tunnel, the longest on the West Coast Main Line at 1 mile and 666yds and the most troublesome engineering work during construction of the original London and Birmingham Railway due to constant flooding. On 30 May 1962, 'Princess Coronation', no. 46240 *City of Coventry* emerges from the southern portal with a Liverpool–Euston express. *(Peter Fitton)*

The north end of Kilsby Tunnel may be seen in the distance as rebuilt 'Patriot', no. 45523 *Bangor*, hauls a train of mixed stock towards Rugby on 9 May 1962. *(Peter Fitton)*

We last saw the 'Royal Scot' at Tring in the hands of a 'Princess Royal' but, having reached Rugby, the train is seen with more usual motive power, namely a 'Princess Coronation', no.46241 *City of Edinburgh*, on Whit Monday, 26 May 1958. The girder bridge behind the train carried the Great Central Railway main line from London Marylebone to Sheffield until its closure in 1966 (ironic as it was the last main line to be built) and the bridge itself was demolished at the end of 2006. *(Michael Mensing)*

Departing south from Rugby on 31 May 1962 is the unique BR 4–6–2, no. 71000 *Duke of Gloucester*, at the head of a Llandudno–Euston express. This was the last express steam locomotive to be built, being completed in 1954, but withdrawn just a few months after this picture was taken. *(Peter Fitton)*

Two 'Princess Coronation' Pacifics grace this busy scene at the north end of the station at 2.56pm on 1 June 1962. On the left is no. 46225 *Duchess of Gloucester* at the head of the 1.20 p.m. Euston–Perth with through coaches for Blackpool Central. It is awaiting signals while sister engine, no. 46237 *City of Bristol*, passes non-stop with a parcels train. On the right is locally based Fairburn 2–6–4 tank, no. 42062, creeping forward on a permanent way train and bearing warning signs at the front of its tanks in connection with the dangers of the electrified wires that would soon reach Rugby. *(Peter Fitton)*

Heading north from Rugby is the pioneer of the Stanier 'Silver Jubilee' class, no. 45552 *Silver Jubilee*, at the front of a football special on 27 January 1962. The supporters were from Arsenal, visiting Manchester United. On the left is the major engineering concern, AEI, a reminder that Rugby was once a very important engineering centre. The only locomotive testing station in Britain was situated beyond the railway shed, shrouded in mist and smoke to the left of the station and beyond the gap in the signals. *(Peter Fitton)*

Rugby to Crewe

North of Rugby the lines to Birmingham veer away to the left, although the Up lines cross the WCML via a flyover. About a half mile beyond the junction the River Avon is crossed, near to the former Newbold water troughs. The Oxford Canal passes under the railway too, before meeting up again and running alongside on the left. The meeting point is by the site of Brinklow station under the famous Roman road, the Fosse Way, that crosses overhead on its course between the Roman towns of Cirencester and Lincoln. Less than 2 miles further on the modern equivalent of the great Roman roads, the M6 motorway, crosses over the line. The canal diverges to the left and just as a cutting is entered we pass the site of Shilton station which, like Brinklow, closed to passengers in 1957. From an embankment the village of Bulkington can be seen on the right with its parish church of St James complete with fourteenth century tower. Its station closed as long ago as 1931. Bedworth, a former coal-mining town that has associations with the writer George Elliot lies to the left. Beyond the next cutting the railway crosses the Ashby-de-la-Zouch Canal.

Lines converge on Nuneaton from Coventry on the left and from Leicester on the right. The station handles cross-country services between Birmingham and East Anglia as well as WCML trains. The former shed at Nuneaton was situated in the fork between the main line and the Coventry branch. The town's textiles and engineering activities together with local quarries would have given plenty of work to the allocation of freight locomotives based here. At the north end of the station the line that branches off to the left is for Birmingham and is of Midland Railway origin. To the right and a little further on is the track bed of another former Midland line, part of which has been restored a few miles away at Market Bosworth. Between Nuneaton and Atherstone the Coventry Canal meanders to the left of the railway while the River Anker pursues its own course on the right. Just beyond the station the dual carriageway A5 crosses over the line for the last time on its way to Holyhead. Both canal and river pass below the line as we approach Polesworth, and beyond this small town, the M42 motorway crosses over the line. On the right, the River Anker opens out to form lakes collectively known as Alvecote Pools. Formed through coal mining subsidence, the lakes are now a nature reserve and designated a Site of Special Scientific Interest, supporting a wide variety of birds, fish and wild flowers.

We pass from Warwickshire into Staffordshire on the approach to Tamworth. On the left is the large tower of the church of St Editha. The name comes from the daughter of Egbert, the first King of England. It is a substantial church due mainly to its being a collegiate foundation and exhibits both Perpendicular and Decorated styles of architecture. At Tamworth the former Midland Railway's north-east to south-west route crosses over the WCML and the high-level station can be seen above Tamworth Low Level. Nearly 3 miles beyond the town we cross the River Tame that wends its way from Birmingham to join the River Trent. Further on, the Birmingham and Fazeley Canal appears alongside the line on the left at Hademore where water troughs were once sited. Approaching Lichfield one can see, on the left, the cathedral's unique sandstone spires, known as 'The Ladies of the Vale'. Parts of the cathedral date back to 700AD while the bulk of the construction was carried out in the twelfth and the fourteenth centuries. Above the station is the cross-country line between Lichfield and Burton.

For much of the next 15 miles to Stafford the dominating feature of the landscape is the wooded upland area of Cannock Chase, which, despite its recreational value, supported the South Staffordshire coalfield. It rises to 800ft at its highest point and contains moorland and forest that was once a hunting ground for Plantaganet kings. Beyond the site of the former station at Armitage (closed 1960) the railway crosses over the Trent and Mersey Canal. A little further on, the River Trent, the third longest river in the country at 170 miles, passes under the railway from right to left where the giant power station and cooling tower of Rugeley will be seen. The branch line that joins on the left is from Walsall. A substantial cutting is negotiated before emerging at Colwich. The remains of the former station building can be seen on the left before passing under the A51 trunk road. The building's shaped gables are typical of the architecture of the North Staffordshire Railway (NSR) and mark the beginning of NSR territory, which branches away to the right; the route to Manchester via Stoke. The NSR was an independent railway until 1923 when it became part of the LMS. Both river and canal follow the route towards Stoke.

The railway cuts through the grounds of Shugborough Park, seat of the Anson family, the Earls of Lichfield. The house dates to 1693 and a member of the family, Admiral Anson, achieved fame for defeating the French in battle in 1747. From the cutting the train enters Shugborough Tunnel which, surprisingly, is the last tunnel encountered by trains on their way to Glasgow. Beyond the tunnel the railway passes the site of Milford and Brocton station (closed in 1960) near to where the Stafford and Worcester canal, on the right, meets the line.

Stafford is approached from the south east via the Queensville curve, beyond which we join the main line from Birmingham and follow the route of the old Grand Junction Railway through Stafford. Immediately north of the station, on the left, is the former locomotive shed, the shell of which remains intact; one of the few steam sheds to survive even in this state. Beyond the engineering works is the truncated line that once ran to Wellington on the GWR network. On the right the track-bed of the former Great Northern Railway branch line to Uttoxeter can be discerned. Apart from an extended siding to Stafford Common the line was closed in 1951. Further away to the left on a hill stands Stafford Castle, a nineteenth-century rebuilding of an earlier castle built on the same site in 1350.

North of the town and beyond the marshes we pass under the M6 motorway and, further on, the site of Great Bridgeford station. About 3 miles beyond the motorway look out on the right for a small, single storey white cottage with thatched roof, close to the railway. This was the birthplace in 1593 and home of the writer Izaak Walton, famous for his book *The Compleat Angler*. The house is now a museum. The island platform at Norton Bridge is the only surviving station between Stafford and Crewe; all the others closed in the 1950s. Just beyond is the junction with the former NSR route to Stoke used by many of the Birmingham–Manchester trains via Stoke.

Just 3 miles beyond Norton Bridge on the right we pass at close quarters the first of two pumping stations. This is the Mill Meece pumping station, built in 1915 and which pumps fresh water from the rocks 300ft below to reservoirs south of Stoke. The station uses electrically-operated submerged pumps but the original steam-powered pumps have been preserved by the Mill Meece Pumping Station Preservation Trust for driving the steam engines. The site of Standon Bridge station is on the north side of the first bridge beyond the pumping station. The railway now runs through heath land, reflecting the underlying rock – Triassic sandstone – prominent in the north-west. The sandstone can be seen more clearly in the cuttings leading to Whitmore where the A53 trunk road crosses over the railway. The site of Whitmore station and the water-troughs lay to the north of the bridge. A little further on, a single-track line joins on the left. It is a spur from the former NSR route from Stoke to Market Drayton and Wellington which lost its passenger service long ago.

The site of Madeley station precedes a series of cuttings followed by an embankment that takes us from Staffordshire into Cheshire and on past the site of Betley Road station. Although barely noticeable, the gradient down to Crewe is the steepest since Camden Bank. It was a gradient that helped the LMS secure a short-lived speed record for steam when Stanier's Coronation reached an official 114mph in 1937. Shortly before milepost 156 the Basford Hall sidings branch out on the left into the marshalling yard which precedes Crewe station. To the right we are joined by the former NSR line from Stoke, while on the left the line from Shrewsbury curves in. At the junction on the left is Crewe motive power depot, built on the site of Crewe South shed, which closed to steam in 1967.

In this fine study of an express locomotive at speed, 'Princess Coronation', no. 46237 *City of Bristol* is seen easing its train, the London-bound 'Royal Scot', towards Rugby on 29 April 1957. It has just taken water from Newbold Troughs and, judging from the activity in the cab, it looks as if the coal is receiving attention. (*Michael Mensing*)

Passing the site of Shilton station on the Trent Valley line, between Rugby and Nuneaton, is a northbound Sunday relief 'Royal Scot' in the hands of 'Princess Coronation', no. 46238 *City of Carlisle*, on 7 April 1963. Shilton station closed in 1957. (*Michael Mensing*)

Nuneaton was, and still is, a busy railway centre, handling traffic on the West Coast Main Line and the intersecting cross-country line between Birmingham and East Anglia. There was once a motive power depot housing a mixture of locomotives for freight as well as local passenger duties. On such a latter duty, a push-pull turn on 7 August 1958, is a Warwick-based Stanier class 2P 0–4–4 tank, no. 41902, probably working the all-stations service to Coventry. Although there were only ten examples of this design they could be seen at various locations along the West Coast Main Line such as Watford, Rugby (where 41902 was allocated for a time), Longsight and Lancaster. (*The Stephenson Locomotive Society*)

At Tamworth Low Level the former Midland main line from the north-east to the south-west crosses over the West Coast Main Line. 'Princess Coronation', no. 46239 *City of Chester* draws admiring glances as it heads northwards with an express. For the trainspotters it was a short distance to the High Level station. (*P. Chancellor Collection*)

On a cold winter's day, instead of the usual Stanier Pacific, 'Royal Scot' 4–6–0, no. 46161 *King's Own* leaves a smoke trail behind as it storms through Tamworth Low Level bound for London in charge of the Up 'Royal Scot' on Saturday 8 March 1958. Peeping from above the canopy on the right is what appears to be a Dutch-style gable, echoing the architecture of the nearby North Staffordshire Railway stations. (*Michael Mensing*)

Lichfield is the next station along the line from Tamworth and also had high and low level platforms. Trainspotters gather by the lineside at Lichfield as 'Princess Royal', no. 46200 *Princess Royal* thunders past with a southbound express in June 1955. The station is beyond the bridge carrying the line from Birmingham and Walsall to Burton-upon-Trent, while the upper station can be seen above the train. (*P. Chancellor Collection*)

A few miles further north of Lichfield, at Colwich, the first of three routes to Manchester veers away to the right. It uses the former North Staffordshire Railway system as far as Macclesfield before rejoining LNWR metals to Manchester. Meanwhile, the West Coast route curves round to the left and enters Shugborough Tunnel below the Earl of Lichfield's estate at Shugborough Hall. The southern portal of this tunnel (the last to be encountered on the journey to Glasgow) can be seen as an unidentified Class 83 passes with an Up train for Euston on 17 August 1974. *(Tom Heavyside)*

Heading north away from the tunnel and passing the site of Milford & Brocton station, is 'Princess Coronation', no. 46241 *City of Edinburgh*, on the Down Sunday 'Royal Scot'. The date is 14 September 1958. (*Michael Mensing*)

Stafford station sees two Stanier Class 5 4–6–0s on an unidentified northbound express. The leading engine is no. 45426, a Longsight engine for a time, so this may be a Manchester-bound express. The identity of the train engine is not known. The station is seen before rebuilding. (*Rex Conway*)

Since Stafford, the route has reverted to four tracks and has followed the original course from London via the Grand Junction Railway's route between Birmingham and the north. The second Manchester branch along former North Staffordshire lines has diverged at Norton Bridge and we are near the site of the next station at Standon Bridge, where a 'Royal Scot', no. 46110 *Grenadier Guardsman*, heads south with the 10.05 a.m. Glasgow–Birmingham on 18 February 1961. (*Hugh Ballantyne*)

Northbound trains follow a rising gradient for about 15 miles from Stafford to Whitmore troughs where a 'Silver Jubilee', no. 45584 *North West Frontier*, is seen on a southbound express on 5 July 1953. From Whitmore to Crewe it is downhill all the way and this falling gradient once allowed the streamlined 'Princess Coronation', no. 6220 *Coronation*, to reach a world record speed, officially given as 114mph, a record that was easily broken by *Mallard* in the following year. (*J.D. Darby*)

For southbound trains from Crewe, the climb to Whitmore requires hard work and a heavy train such as 'The Comet', from Manchester to Euston, needs a locomotive in good shape to keep to time. Longsight-based 'Royal Scot', no. 46129 *The Scottish Horse*, seems up to the job as it climbs Madeley Bank on 30 September 1951. *(J.D. Darby)*

Another climb up Madeley Bank is being made by ex-LNWR 0–8–0, no. 9196, in charge of a mixed freight. It appears to be struggling as it makes its ascent on 18 August 1946. *(J.D. Darby)*

Traditional motive power is seen at the head of the 'Royal Scot' as 'Princess Coronation' no. 46226 *Duchess of Norfolk* passes the remains of Betley Road station on 17 September 1956. The station closed to passengers in 1945 and completely in 1950. *(Ron Gee)*

A scene almost reminiscent of some of the Reverend Awdry's images is depicted near Betley Road, as an ex-Midland Railway 2F 0–6–0, no. 58196, potters about the goods yard on 17 September 1956. *(Ron Gee)*

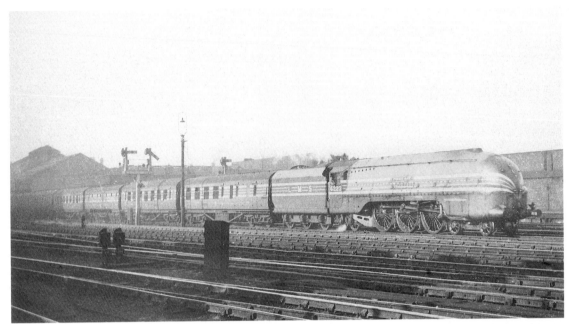

A scene from the glory days of the LMS as streamlined 'Princess Coronation', no. 6223 *Princess Alice*, in blue and white and ushered forward by LNWR signals, runs non-stop through Crewe with the southbound 'Coronation Scot' on 2 September 1938. *(J.D. Darby)*

Apart from being the largest railway centre on the West Coast Main Line with two substantial motive power depots plus a third smaller shed at Gresty Lane, Crewe was home to a major railway works where many of the locomotives seen on this route were built or maintained. It was also a junction for trains from Manchester, Chester and North Wales, Stoke and Shrewsbury. Great Western locomotives were a daily sight here and on 2 September 1938 a GWR 2–6–2 tank, no. 5142, arrives with what is thought to be the 10.30 a.m. Portsmouth–Manchester London Road (now Piccadilly). *(J.D. Darby)*

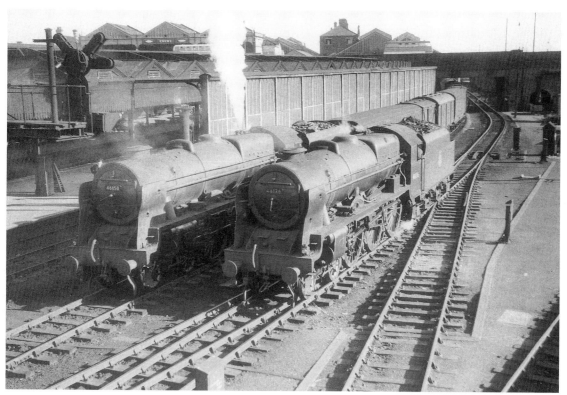

Two 'Royal Scots' pose at the north end of Crewe station whose road entrance can be seen above the loco on the left. No. 46150 *The Life Guardsman* awaits the right away with a parcels train. Next to no. 46150 is no. 46136 *The Border Regiment* awaiting its next turn. (*www.transporttreasury.co.uk*)

Another view of the 'Royal Scot' as it approaches Crewe station from the north behind 'Princess Coronation', no. 46220 *Coronation*, on 11 July 1953. The lines veering away to the left lead to Chester and North Wales as well as Crewe Works. (*J.D. Darby*)

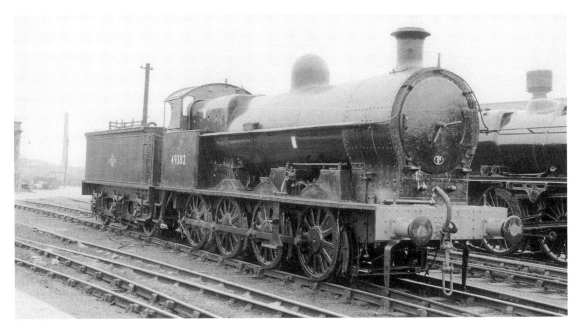

While at Crewe it is worth making a brief visit to Crewe Works where ex-LNWR 0–8–0, no. 49382, from Preston shed has been newly outshopped at its birthplace and stands in the works yard. The date is 2 October 1960, nine months before a severe fire at Preston shed in June 1961 would destroy the roof and also damage a number of locomotives, including no. 49382. *(Hugh Ballantyne)*

Crewe North shed housed several of the 'Princess Coronation' class and on 21 July 1964, when this picture was taken, it was home to no. 46256 *Sir William A. Stanier*, named after the designer of these locomotives. No. 46256 was built in 1947 with modifications and detail differences from earlier members of the class. The coaling plant at the depot is prominent in the background. Crewe North closed in 1965 but by then the 'Princess Coronation' Pacifics had all been withdrawn, no. 46256 being the last to go in October 1964 following its use on some special trains. *(Peter Fitton)*

Crewe to Preston

eaving Crewe we pass the site, on the left, of Crewe North depot which closed in 1965. It was one of the principal depots for maintaining the top-link steam locomotives. Crewe Works is situated further along the Chester and Holyhead line that curves away to the left. Veering off to the right are the lines to Manchester. The LNWR constructed cuttings below the main line to allow the movement of freight to cross the path of passenger trains without disruption. However, until 1985 when the track-work was rationalised, all trains were subject to a severe speed restriction through the station. North of the Holyhead junction on the left is the Crewe Heritage Centre where the Advanced Passenger Train of the 1970s is prominently displayed. It was a train that promised to revolutionise WCML services and achieved a British record for speed.

Rolling north over the Cheshire Plain, populated by Friesian dairy cattle, we pass the site of Minshull Vernon station (closed 1942) in between two cuttings about 5 miles north of Crewe. Beyond the second cutting the Shropshire Union Canal is crossed as it makes its way towards Middlewich over to the right. The word 'wich' incidentally is the old word for a brine well. Although we have now reached the large salt mining area of Winsford, Middlewich and Northwich, there is very little evidence of this major industry that is actually visible from the train. Today, rock salt is almost entirely extracted as brine by pumping water into the beds to dissolve the salt. Much of this product is used in the manufacture of chemicals at Northwich, Runcorn and Widnes. Winsford station is situated at the beginning of a cutting and further cuttings lead us to Hartford station and beyond. The former Cheshire Lines Committee route from Manchester to Chester crosses over the main line, less than half a mile north west of the station, and a spur from this line joins the WCML on the right, north of the bridge. The spur is primarily used by freight traffic. Beyond Acton Bridge station and between further cuttings, we cross the river Weaver on the Dutton Viaduct. It is of stone and composed of twenty arches. At Weaver Junction the lines diverge left and right for Liverpool. The Up Liverpool line on the right crosses over the WCML via a flyover which is said to be the first of its type in the world.

The line now passes through another cutting, at the far end of which lies the site of Preston Brook station (closed 1958), immediately before the first of two bridges in quick succession. The second bridge carries the M56 motorway between Chester and Greater Manchester. Immediately beyond, the historic Bridgewater Canal may be glimpsed on the right, close to its junction with the Trent and Mersey Canal. On the hill to the left is a tower that may look like a folly but is in fact a water tower built for Liverpool Corporation in 1892. Crossing over the main line a little further on is the former Birkenhead Joint (GWR and LNWR) Railway. It is the principal route from Wales to the North of England and merges with the WCML just south of Warrington at Acton Grange Junction. The sites of Moore troughs and the station of the same name (closed 1943) lay beyond the railway bridge. The mysterious white tower that can be seen on the right is the Daresbury research laboratory.

Beyond Acton Grange Junction the Manchester Ship Canal and River Mersey are crossed in quick succession. The historic canal was completed in 1894 and was once an essential ingredient in the economic growth of Manchester. However, it has now largely outlived its initial purpose and most ships now travel inland as far as Ellesmere Port. Over to the left is the large power station at Fiddlers Ferry on the banks of the Mersey. It is a visible sign of the industrial North, the face of which changed considerably in only a short time. The colliery wheels have gone and mill chimneys are hard to find. Approaching Warrington it should be possible to see the prominent 281-feet high spire of the parish church of St Elphin on the right. Warrington station (formerly Bank Quay) is dominated by the large soap factory on the left. One of the reasons for this location was its proximity to the salt industry in Cheshire. There was once a Low Level station under the south end of the main line platforms but it closed in 1962.

North of the station, the WCML is crossed by two road bridges and the CLC route between Manchester and Liverpool. The site of the locomotive depot at Warrington Dallam was situated a little further on the left. Having passed under the M62 motorway, about 2 miles north of Warrington, we approach Winwick Junction. Since Warrington we have travelled over the oldest part of the WCML, built in 1831 for the Warrington and Newton Railway between Earlestown Junction (then known as Newton) and Warrington. It was the southerly extension of the historic Liverpool and Manchester Railway. The modern WCML veers to the right along a cut-off route towards Golborne. At this point we pass briefly into the County of Merseyside from Cheshire. Vulcan village lies to the left where there was a long tradition of locomotive building. The works have now gone but many diesel locomotives associated with the WCML were built here including pioneer diesel, no. 10000, the Class 40s and 50s, as well as the famous Deltic diesels of the East Coast Main Line. The works was established in 1845 with Robert Stephenson as an original partner.

The railway enters a long cutting during which it passes under the old Liverpool and Manchester Railway and under the M6 before reaching Golborne Junction where a spur from the Liverpool and Manchester Railway joins on the right. From here, this section of the formative WCML reached Wigan in 1832 and Preston in 1838. At Golborne Junction we pass from Merseyside into Greater Manchester, two counties that have absorbed much of what was South Lancashire. The town of Golborne appears on either side before the line passes into a cutting. Its station closed in 1961. About 2 miles further along the line, the site of Bamfurlong station (closed 1960) is passed immediately before the A58 trunk road crosses overhead. Beyond the bridge we cross the Leigh branch of the Leeds and Liverpool Canal, built for the transportation of coal but now used for leisure purposes. There are two junctions on the left with lines leading to and from St Helens while opposite the second junction is the site of the former Springs Branch locomotive shed on the right. Passing through a cutting on the approach to Wigan we cross the Leeds and Liverpool Canal while on the right is the line from Manchester.

At one time, the Wigan area probably had a more complex network of railways, including industrial lines, than anywhere else along the WCML. Most of this network closed following the declining fortunes of the local coal industry.

A few mills still exist in Wigan including Trencherfield Mill, seen on the left on the approach to the station. It has a pyramidal top to its tower. It was built in 1907 and stands close to Wigan 'Pier'. Over to the right is the stubby tower of the parish church in the town centre before we pass through Wigan North Western. The town once possessed three stations of which two survive. North of the main line station, Wigan Wallgate station can be seen on the right below the WCML. It handles passenger trains from Manchester to Southport and Merseyside. The lines to these destinations can be seen separating on the left-hand side. This is mainly former L&YR territory and most of the lines operating in this area between Wigan and Preston were once part of the LYR system. The railway passes above the town before entering a cutting. At the far end of this cutting a road bridge crosses above the line just before the site of Boars Head station, where a branch line veered away to the right towards Chorley and Blackburn. About a mile further on there was another junction station at Standish that, like Boars Head, closed in 1949. Here, lines that avoided Wigan joined from the right. They were used by both freight and passenger trains, especially summer excursions to Blackpool, routed this way around Wigan to avoid congestion on the WCML. Many of the lines that exist as track-beds in this area fell victim to the closure boom of the 1960s.

Between two cuttings we enter modern Lancashire, more rural altogether than the old county. However, a reminder of old Lancashire can be seen on the left as we pass the Coppull Ring Mills of red brick with tower and cupola. They were built in 1906. There was a station nearby but it closed in 1969. A further three miles along the line Balshaw Lane station suffered the same fate but has since been replaced by a new station. Winter Hill can be seen in the distance to the right. It is just under 1,500ft high, with a television mast on top. On the left side is the West Lancashire Plain, noted for its production of vegetables due to the draining of mosses and peat bogs that have provided light, peaty soils, suitable for the growth of such crops.

On the right we are joined by the main line from Manchester to Preston and Blackpool. It is a former LYR route. Both the LYR and LNWR competed for the Blackpool traffic, and they shared responsibility for this section of the line to Preston and to Blackpool. Between Euxton Junction and Preston was the only section of the WCML up to Carlisle not exclusively operated by the LNWR but under joint administration. Beyond the M6 motorway, which crosses over the line, a cutting is entered leading us to Leyland and its station. The town is well-known for its former British Leyland motor complex specialising in commercial vehicles and which can be seen on the left a mile north of the station. Lines diverging to the right lead towards Lostock Hall and Blackburn. Beyond the site of Farington station the Blackburn line crosses over the WCML and then curves round to join the WCML at Farington Curve Junction, used also by local trains to and from Ormskirk.

Beyond the cutting and Skew Bridge the vista opens out as we approach Preston. On the right the old route from Blackburn is now a trackless course that crosses the River Ribble about a quarter of a mile away. Once across the Ribble, the former Park Hotel appears on the right. Jointly built by the LYR and LNWR in 1882 it is now used as offices. It is red brick with a tower and pyramidal roof.

The journey resumes northwards from Crewe having left the Chester and Manchester branches behind. At Coppenhall Junction the 2.25 p.m. Morecambe–Crewe with a clean looking 'Royal Scot', no. 46157 *The Royal Artilleryman*, in charge, nears the end of its trip at the head of the lightweight train on 30 May 1961. *(John Hilton)*

The rebuilt Winsford station was preparing for the inauguration of electric services between Liverpool and Crewe when this picture was taken of 'Silver Jubilee', no. 45634 *Trinidad*, leaving Winsford station with the 6.10 a.m. Carlisle–Crewe stopping service on 16 February 1962. The locomotive was based at Crewe South at the time. *(John Hilton)*

Following the passage of a Down train seen in the distance, Hartford station receives another visitor in the form of 'Princess Coronation', no. 46241 *City of Edinburgh*, racing through with a lengthy Glasgow–Birmingham express on 13 April 1962. *(John Hilton)*

A little further north from Hartford, the West Coast Main Line passes under the former Cheshire Lines Committee route between Manchester and Chester. There is a connection between the two lines used primarily by freight trains including those serving the salt and chemical industries based in the area of Winsford and Northwich. The connecting lines and sidings can be seen in the background as the 10.58 a.m. London–Blackpool express heads northwards behind 'Royal Scot', no. 46154 *The Hussar* on 26 September 1957. *(John Hilton)*

Works are under way at Acton Bridge, including the provision of a new signal-box, in readiness for electrification as the 'Royal Scot' passes on its way to Euston behind 'Princess Coronation', no. 46245 *City of London* on 18 June1960. Note the busy station yard. *(John Hilton)*

Less than a year later, the gantries and wires are up as the 1.40 p.m. Birmingham–Liverpool express approaches from the south. At the head of the train on 24 May 1961 is an unnamed example of one of the unrebuilt 'Patriots', no. 45551, with a high-sided tender. In the loop line, waiting for a passage north, is an LNWR 0–8–0 designed by Bowen-Cooke. *(John Hilton)*

Before leaving Acton Bridge, we see an unusual visitor in the shape of Midland Railway 3F 0–6–0, no. 43340, from Burton shed on 18 June 1960. *(D. Chatfield)*

At Weaver Junction the lines to Liverpool split from the main line. Seen passing the junction on 12 April 1953 is an LMS 2–6–0, no.42937, designed by George Hughes and familiarly known as a 'Crab'. Although nearly 250 of these engines were built in the 1920s, relatively few of the West Coast Main Line depots had allocations of them. *(J.D. Darby)*

Beyond Weaver Junction the line passes through a cutting and it is here that we see the southbound 'Royal Scot' at Preston Brook behind 'Princess Coronation', no. 46256 *Sir William A. Stanier F.R.S.*, of Camden depot on 4 August 1958. *(Gavin Morrison)*

About a mile north of the cutting the main lines passes beneath the Chester to Manchester route, via Warrington and Earlestown, before the two lines meet on the approach to Warrington. A Stanier 2–6–0, no. 42970, has just passed below the Chester to Manchester line, south of Moore, on its way south with a freight on 31 August 1963. Unlike the numerous Hughes 2–6–0s, the Stanier version comprised just forty engines. *(Peter Fitton)*

Although this picture is taken at the dawn of nationalisation, there is still an LMS feel conveyed by 'Princess Coronation' no. 6253 *City of St Albans* as it picks up water at Moore Troughs while heading south with the 'Royal Scot' on 15 May 1948. The service had only recently been reintroduced after the war when this picture was taken but it would be some time before the headboard would be added. The boy on the left has rolled up his trousers in anticipation of a wetting. (*J.D. Darby*)

In the opposite direction, two decades later, a Stanier Class 5 4–6–0, no. 44838, takes on water while passing over Moore Troughs with an unidentified northbound express in the then new blue and grey livery on 28 May 1966. In the distance is the water tower serving the Runcorn area, while in the bottom left-hand corner is a cast iron London and North Western Railway warning sign. (*Hugh Ballantyne*)

Having crossed the Manchester Ship Canal and the River Mersey we arrive at Warrington, where a very dirty 'Princess Coronation' no. 46228 *Duchess of Rutland* passes through Bank Quay station with the 'Mid-day Scot' in 1951. Given the lack of attention paid to the locomotive it is surprising that anyone should go to the trouble of chalking the name of the train on the smokebox door. *(www.transporttreasury.co.uk)*

Warrington's main line motive power depot, Dallam, was at the north end of the town, and on 25 September 1960 it played host to a visiting unrebuilt 'Patriot', no. 45505 *Royal Army Ordnance Corps*, from Carlisle Upperby depot. Some of the unrebuilt members of this class, such as no. 45505, were paired with high-sided tenders. *(Hugh Ballantyne)*

Since leaving Warrington the journey has been along the oldest part of the route, dating back almost to the beginning of the railway age, at least on the main line. From the oldest main line, the Liverpool and Manchester Railway, further lines were connected to form the beginnings of a railway network. Wigan to the north and Warrington to the south were the first towns to be reached. When the West Coast Main line was completed throughout, the route incorporated part of the Liverpool and Manchester Railway between Earlestown and Parkside, two of the oldest junctions. Many years later, when under the control of the London & North Western Railway, a cut-off route was built to speed up services and reduce congestion. The new line ran from Winwick to Golborne where new junctions were created. In this picture of Winwick Junction on Lancashire's mossland, an unnamed 'Patriot', no. 45544, is crossing the main line from the Earlestown line having had to wait for the Down 'Mid-day Scot' to clear the junction on 1 April 1960. (*Hugh Ballantyne*)

Looking in the opposite direction to the photograph on page 75, we see a Stanier 8F 2–8–0, no. 48307, with a Down engineers' train on 28 August 1965 approaching Winwick Junction. *(Hugh Ballantyne)*

At the southern end of the Lancashire coalfield we see BR 'Britannia', no. 70031, minus its nameplates (formerly *Byron*) passing Golborne with a Carlisle–Crewe parcels train on 23 April 1966. Between here and north of Wigan there lay a dense network of lines. Many of these lines were industrial, serving mines and factories, and were operated by privately-owned locomotives. However, today virtually nothing survives of the complex railway network around Wigan. *(Peter Fitton)*

A Stanier Class 5 4–6–0, no. 45305, stands in the bay platform of Wigan North Western with the 5.35 p.m. to Warrington on 15 April 1966. Happily, this locomotive can be seen today following its preservation. (*Peter Fitton*)

The 'Royal Scot' is seen in the diesel era as a pair of Class 50s, nos 435 and 423, pass Bradley, just north of Standish Junction, on 16 August 1971. The slow lines on the right were abandoned during electrification work. Standish Junction provided a connection to the main line for the Wigan avoiding lines, used mainly by freight and excursion trains. (*Tom Heavyside*)

There was less than a year to go before the end of steam on British Railways when this picture was taken in the cutting at Charnock Richard. BR class 9F, no. 92017, heads north with a Widnes–Long Meg (on the Settle & Carlisle) empties on 23 August 1967. *(Peter Fitton)*

This Aspinall 3F 0–6–0, no. 52105, seen at Charnock Richard in June 1951, is a reminder that between Wigan and Preston the journey is passing through Lancashire & Yorkshire Railway territory, stretching from Southport in the west to Yorkshire in the east. Note the wooden-bodied wagons. *(F. & R. Hewitt courtesy of the Stephenson Locomotive Society)*

Just south of Euxton Junction an unrebuilt 'Royal Scot', no. 46158 *The Loyal Regiment*, heads southwards with fruit empties on 7 July 1949. *(Ron Gee)*

A 'Silver Jubilee', no. 45571 *South Africa* is seen approaching Euxton Junction from the north. It is at the head of the 9.15 a.m. Blackpool Central–Manchester Victoria train on 12 October 1963 and will leave the West Coast Main Line at the junction to take the Manchester line via Chorley and Bolton. *(Peter Fitton)*

North of Euxton Junction the West Coast Main Line was once jointly owned by the LNWR and Lancashire and Yorkshire Railway under the title of the North Union Joint Railway as far as Preston. North of Leyland, this scene is at Farington Junction and shows two expresses at a standstill. English Electric Type 4, no. D317, is at the head of the London–Perth on the slow line while sister engine, no. D337, waits with a Birmingham–Glasgow and Edinburgh express and would later be forced to reverse and take the curve to the right towards Lostock Hall. Coming off the curve is rebuilt 'Patriot', no. 45534 *E. Tootal Broadhurst* with empty coaching stock. The cause of the delay is not known. The bridge spanning the West Coast Main Line in the distance carries the former Lancashire and Yorkshire route from Preston and East Lancashire to Liverpool. Over to the right, the tower of the coaling plant is visible at Lostock motive power depot, one of the last three sheds to survive at the end of the steam era. *(Peter Fitton)*

Beyond the bridge seen in the distance in the previous picture, the West Coast Main Line enters a cutting and is joined by lines from Liverpool and East Lancashire at Farington Curve Junction. Here seen approaching this junction from the north is a Stanier 2–6–4 tank, no. 42456, on the 12.20 p.m. local to Wigan North Western on 4 April 1964. Just visible in the background is the edge of Skew Bridge. *(Peter Fitton)*

Skew Bridge is in the background of this picture as 'Princess Coronation', no. 46229 *Duchess of Hamilton*, at the head of 'The Lakes Express', emerges from the cutting and approaches Preston on 26 August 1961. The fourteen-coach express appears to be composed mainly of LMS stock. *(Peter Fitton)*

Skew Bridge signal-box is approached from the north by ex-LNWR 0–8–0, no. 49141, in ex-works condition, on a trip working on 3 September 1959. The picture has been taken from an overtaking train. *(Peter Fitton)*

This BR class 9F 2–10–0, no. 92249, has just crossed the River Ribble and is approaching Skew Bridge from the Preston direction as it heads southbound with empties on 9 November 1963. *(Peter Fitton)*

Another arrival at Preston from the south. 'Silver Jubilee', no. 45642 *Boscawen*, with Fowler tender, brings an express under an array of signals into the station. One of the local allocation of 'Jinties' is seen on the right, probably on station pilot duties. *(RAS Marketing)*

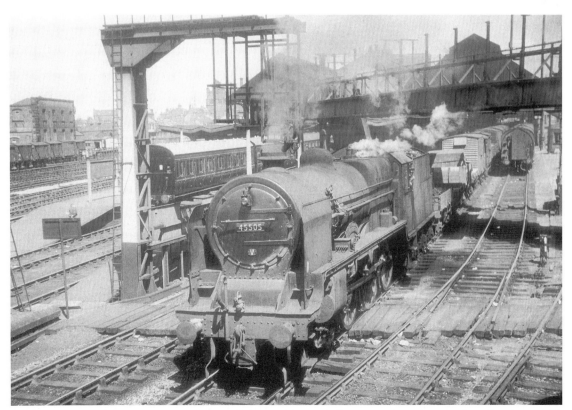

We last saw 'Patriot', no. 45505 *Royal Army Ordnance Corps*, at Warrington, but now we see it heading south out of Preston station with an Up freight on 27 June 1961. This picture gives only a partial idea of the size of this station as the East Lancashire section (demolished in the 1960s) over to the right cannot be seen. *(Peter Fitton)*

This picture, taken from the station platform, shows 'Princess Coronation', no. 46250 *City of Lichfield* in excellent external condition, taking the through Down line to the west of the station with a freight on 19 October 1963. Just beyond the front of the locomotive, a line drops down on a sharp gradient towards the docks. *(Peter Fitton)*

Work-stained Stanier Class 5 4-6-0, no.45201, arrives at Preston's platform 9 with the 12.20 p.m. Blackpool Central–Liverpool Exchange on 20 February 1963. While it is possible still to travel by train from Blackpool to Liverpool, subsequent rationalisation has made the journey of this particular train impossible as both termini at Blackpool and Liverpool have disappeared and Preston's East Lancashire platforms, used by this train, have also gone. *(Peter Fitton)*

Preston to Tebay

From Preston station we immediately pass under Fishergate, one of the oldest of Preston's streets. After the bridge there are sidings to the right in an area that was dominated by the Lancaster Canal before it was cut back to a point about a mile north. Beyond the sidings the County Sessions Hall of 1903, with its tower 170ft high and of several tiers, is prominent. In the distance, on the same side, the modern superstructure of Preston North End's football stadium may be seen.

On the left, before the branch for Blackpool, is Preston power box, on the site of Preston motive power depot, which was substantially destroyed by fire in 1961. On the opposite side of the track are the remains of the former branch line to Longridge. It was progressively cut back until closure in 1980 except for a short section to Deepdale Junction. In between the Blackpool line and the WCML is the church of St Walburge, a landmark in the area. Its almost ghostly steeple of light grey limestone is 303ft high and was designed by Hansom, inventor of the Hansom Cab. Former textile mills can be seen on the left before we enter a series of cuttings that take us through the northern suburbs of Preston. Just before emerging from the cuttings we pass under the M55 motorway to Blackpool.

Look out for the M6 appearing on the right and keeping company with the railway for about 5 miles. Passing the sites of Brock station and the water-troughs, the railway and motorway are joined briefly by the A6 trunk road and Lancaster Canal within a narrow half-mile band. The canal meanders alongside the left-hand side of the railway and beyond the point where it veers away, the track-bed of the former branch line to Knott End may be identified on the left. It appears at the site of Garstang and Catterall station that closed in 1969, the last of the intermediate stations between Preston and Lancaster to close; Barton and Broughton, Brock, Scorton and Galgate all closed as long ago as 1939 while Bay Horse lost its services in 1960.

Since Preston we have been running to the east of the area known as the Fylde, while on the right are the most southerly of the numerous fells that are encountered for the remainder of the journey in England. Much of the underlying rock strata to the east is Millstone Grit (the formation that underlies much of the Pennines), and, containing little lime, provides the soft water which was essential for the cotton industry in Lancashire. Millstone Grit has been a good solid building material for much of the North of England.

Where the motorway veers away to the right we pass the village of Scorton and, a little further on, the railway crosses over the River Wyre heading westwards towards the sea at Fleetwood. Beyond the cuttings the motorway draws nearer to the railway and the distinctive shape of Forton service station can be seen to the right on the M6.

The railway crosses over the A6 trunk road at the village of Galgate. A little further on, the A6 runs alongside the railway for more than 2 miles, during which the modern campus at Lancaster University can be seen on the right. The historic city of Lancaster is approached via cuttings and the crossing of the Lancaster Canal. The station was known once as Lancaster Castle because of the proximity of the castle above the station on the right. Part of the station buildings mimic the architecture of the castle which is medieval with a Norman keep. Next to the castle is the priory and church of St Mary which is believed to date back in part to Saxon times. Immediately on the left beyond the station is the track-bed of the branch to Glasson Dock which closed in the 1960s, while to the right was the connection to Lancaster Green Ayre with its locomotive depot on the former Midland Railway.

Leaving Lancaster there are further views back to the right of the castle and look out for St Peter's, the Catholic Cathedral, with a splendid 240ft steeple. Further away is the large green-domed building known as the Ashton Memorial, built for Lord Ashton in memory of his wife. It was completed in 1909, stands 175ft high and is regarded as one of the grandest monuments in England. Old warehouses can be seen on the south bank of the River Lune while on the north bank a riverside path marks the track-bed of the former Midland route to Morecambe. The triangular junction for Morecambe appears on the left about 2 miles north of Lancaster and then we get one brief glimpse of the west coast in the form of Morecambe Bay, which can in fact be crossed on foot at low tide, but only with guides. Across the bay lies Grange-over-Sands and beyond are the lower hills of the Lake District. Morecambe Bay is a very important estuary for both resident and migrating birds. Stations at Hest Bank, located by one of the few remaining traditional signal boxes, and Bolton-le-Sands were closed in 1969. Water troughs were situated at Hest Bank.

The A6 and the Lancaster Canal briefly make contact with the railway on the right as we approach Carnforth, a town that developed with the railways. On the left is the former Carnforth motive power depot, one of the last three to have an allocation of steam locomotives in August 1968. The large concrete structure which towers over the yard is the coaling plant. This centre is Steamtown and repairs preserved steam locomotives. The main line platforms of Carnforth station have disappeared but the branch line platforms for Barrow and the Cumbrian coast services still survive together with the tea room used in the famous film, *Brief Encounter*. This station marks the beginning of the Furness Railway system to Barrow and Whitehaven. Beyond the station the line passes under the joint Furness & Midland Railway route between Leeds and Morecambe.

The Lancaster Canal runs alongside the railway on the right about 3 miles north of Carnforth and where it veers away is the border from Lancashire into what used to be Westmorland but is now Cumbria. Weather permitting, it is possible to see some of the large mountains of the Lake District on the left including Old Man of Coniston which is associated with the quarrying of slate. Many roofs in the Lake District are tiled with green Westmorland slate. The sites of the former stations at Burton and Holme, and Milnthorpe may be identified, together with the track-bed of an ex-Furness Railway branch on the left at Hincaster Junction, 2 miles beyond Milnthorpe. The hill on the right as we approach Oxenholme is known as The Helm, 608ft at its highest point and containing the earthworks of an ancient hillfort.

At Oxenholme station the former LNWR branch line to Kendal and Windermere, 10 miles away, branches away to the left. Once used by express trains such as 'The Lakes Express', this line now supports mainly diesel multiple units. Through the cutting beyond the station, look left for a view of Kendal in the Kent Valley. Visible from the line is the Norman castle of Kendal, situated on a low hill, where Katherine Parr, Henry VIII's sixth wife, was born and spent her childhood.

Now under the shadow of Hay Fell on the right, one can catch a further glimpse of some of the larger mountains in the Lake District on a clear day by looking to the left. In the distance the Langdale Pikes may be visible. The word 'fell' is found mainly in the northern counties because it was here where Danes and Norwegians settled and this word of Scandinavian origin means large hill or small mountain. Likewise, the word 'thorpe' (meaning hamlet) as in Milnthorpe, south of Oxenholme, and 'beck', which is the word used to describe many of the local streams, are of Scandinavian origin.

The line swings sharply to the right so that it faces eastwards, following the valley of the River Mint, down below on the left, seen to good effect from Docker viaduct. Beyond the site of

Grayrigg station we pass under the M6, which was opened in this area in 1970. Looking to the right we should see the attractive stone Low Gill viaduct that once carried the former LNWR line that served Sedburgh, Kirkby Lonsdale and Ingleton. Beyond the viaduct is the Lune Valley and now as the railway changes course again towards the north it joins the river and the motorway to pass through the narrow Lune gorge hemmed in by the hills, passing the site of Low Gill station. This is the beginning of possibly the most popular stretch of railway line in the country among railway photographers during the steam era. It was the ideal setting to see the steam locomotive working hard against the gradient and the elements but nowadays the names of Dillicar troughs, Tebay, Scout Green and Shap have lost their magic.

The hills that tower over us on the right are the attractive grass-covered Howgill Fells. The site of Dillicar water troughs is located near to Tebay, a village of grey stone houses lining the road on the hill to the right. They were built for railway workers in the 1840s. The former station and locomotive depot on the left, which supplied banking engines for many of the trains making the ascent of Shap, closed in 1968. Beyond the station, the North Eastern Railway's route over the Pennines to Darlington branched away to the right. The route was notorious for its snow drifts, capable of blocking a train's path for days.

The departure north from Preston is impressive for two reasons. The remarkable signal gantry has been used many times by photographers to compose a picture, while the thin spire of St Walburge remains a familiar landmark to this day. Below the left-hand side of the gantry can be seen no. 5 signal-box at Preston. BR Class 2 2–6–2 tank, no. 84018, will cut across to the left, beyond the gantry, in order to take the line for Blackpool Central which curves away to the left, in front of the church. *(Tony Bretherton, Peter Fitton Collection)*

Passing No. 5 signal-box, 'Royal Scot', no. 46107 *Argyll and Sutherland Highlander*, struggles to lift a heavy Manchester/Liverpool–Glasgow/Edinburgh express up the gradient and out of Preston on 26 November 1961. The Blackpool lines can be seen cutting across the main line as the afternoon sun in the west casts light on the ensemble. *(Peter Fitton)*

Beyond the junction for Blackpool the West Coast Main Line reverts to two tracks through the northern suburbs of Preston. Drifting passed Oxheys signal-box is 'Silver Jubilee', no. 45721 *Impregnable*, at the head of the Up 'Lakes Express' on 29 August 1963. In the background are the chimneys of the local textile mills. Note the milepost on the left indicating the distance from Preston. The mileposts revert to '0' at four points along the route for historical reasons based on the building of the West Coast Main Line by different companies. The mileposts change at Golborne Junction, Preston, Lancaster and Carlisle. *(Peter Fitton)*

The Lancashire fells form a backcloth in this view of 'Princess Coronation', no. 46244 *King George VI*, seen collecting water from Brock Troughs while in charge of the southbound Glasgow–Birmingham express on 22 July 1960. The M6 now runs alongside to the right of the railway at this point. *(Peter Fitton)*

Garstang & Catterall station lay roughly half way between Preston and Lancaster, and is visited briefly on 30 June 1964 by BR Class 4 2–6–0, no.76083, in charge of an Up mixed freight. Beyond the station is the creamery, while the bay platform once accommodated trains for Garstang Town and the Lancashire coast at Knott End. However, the passenger service along that branch was abandoned as long ago as 1930. The left-hand arch of the distant railway bridge accommodated the branch line. The station was the last to close between Preston and Lancaster in 1969. *(Peter Fitton)*

Lancaster Castle
overlooks the
approach to this city
from the south as
WD 2–8–0, no. 90346,
ventures south with a
track train on
30 August 1964.
(Peter Fitton)

At the north end of Lancaster Castle station, 'Princess Coronation', no. 46254 *City of Stoke on Trent* hurries 'The Royal Scot' southwards on 8 September 1963, a late date to see these engines with the 'Royal Scot' headboard. The branch on the right leads to Lancaster Green Ayre where there was a steam depot until 1966. The overhead wires were used by electric multiple units operating between Lancaster and Morecambe. *(Peter Fitton)*

At Hest Bank a 'Royal Scot' 4–6–0, no. 46129 *The Scottish Horse*, is unusually in charge of the Down 'Royal Scot' express on 15 October 1951. These locomotives had regular Sunday turns on this express at times during the 1950s but on this occasion the 'Royal Scot' is seen on a weekday. *(B. Hilton, www.transporttreasury.co.uk)*

Cattle poke their noses out of a wagon as BR Class 4 4–6–0, no. 75015, ambles towards Hest Bank station on 3 August 1967. Beyond the train Morecambe Bay stretches away with the lower hills of the Lake District in the distance. Presumably the term 'West Coast Main Line' originated as a marketing slogan, as it is stretching things to describe this route as such when the only point that can be seriously treated as the west coast is here at Morecambe Bay. (*Tom Heavyside*)

Morecambe can be seen across the bay on the right as Hest Bank station receives a visitor on 3 August 1967 in the form of BR 'Britannia', no. 70010, reduced to humble duties such as the haulage of two parcels vans from Lancaster. The old world looks as if it might carry on for ever but the sight of such an engine on lowly duties and the absence of its nameplates (it was formerly *Owen Glendower*) are pointers to decline. In fact, the whole scene would soon change. The camping coaches, a familiar sight at some seaside locations, along with the wagons in the station yard would soon disappear. The sidings and eventually the station would follow into oblivion after closure in 1969. (*Tom Heavyside*)

Hest Bank Troughs lay between Hest Bank station and Bolton-le-Sands, through which the 'Royal Scot' passes on its southbound journey behind 'Princess Coronation' no. 46237 *City of Bristol* on 6 August 1955. (*R. Butterfield/Initial Photographics*)

Carnforth marked the beginning of the Furness Railway network, stretching around the coast to Whitehaven. In this view of Carnforth, from the south on 30 August 1964, the former Furness Railway platforms are situated to the left of the main line. The tea room on the centre platform achieved fame as the setting for part of the film *Brief Encounter*. Slowing for a signal stop on the main line is rebuilt 'Patriot', no. 45531 *Sir Frederick Harrison*, with milk vans for the south. In a few minutes the northbound 'Mid-Day Scot' will pass by with *City of Stoke-on-Trent* in charge. (*Peter Fitton*)

A Stanier Class 5 4–6–0 on the 'Royal Scot' was a comparative rarity but they were used many times, more usually in pairs, when in charge of the diverted train or, as in this case, when the designated loco has failed. On this occasion, 'Princess Coronation', no. 46223 *Princess Alice* had to be removed at Carnforth. A Preston-based 'Class 5', no. 45332, was on hand and is seen ready to resume the journey complete with headboard on 1 September 1960. *(Peter Fitton)*

At the north end of Carnforth the 'Royal Scot' approaches from the north behind 'Princess Coronation', no. 46254 *City of Stoke-on-Trent* on 2 August 1964, a very late date for haulage by this class of locomotive on the premier train. Bearing in mind that the 'Princess Coronation' class were all withdrawn by 12 September except for no. 46256, could this have been the last pairing of these engines with the 'Royal Scot'? In the distance the overhead bridge carries the former Furness & Midland Joint Railway towards Yorkshire. *(Peter Fitton)*

The coaling tower of Carnforth shed can be seen in the background as Fowler 4F 0–6–0, no. 44276, accelerates its ballast train away from the station, past a storage depot, and northwards into the hills on 30 August 1964. For most of the next 30 miles the journey is uphill with some of the steepest gradients encountered so far. *(Peter Fitton)*

The north end of Oxenholme is seen in this view of 'Royal Scot', no.46166 *London Rifle Brigade*, below an LNWR signal, departing with the Crewe–Carlisle parcels train at 12.22 p.m. on 23 July 1963. The Windermere branch trains use the bay platform immediately in front of the slate wall. The locomotive depot at Oxenholme had closed the previous year. *(Peter Fitton)*

The cattle appear to be unmoved by the passage of Stanier 8F 2–8–0, no. 48472, on an Up freight on 25 July 1963. The wagons at the rear of the train are crossing Docker Viaduct and in the background are the Howgill Fells. For this train it is downhill most of the way to Carnforth. *(Peter Fitton)*

The gradient is unrelenting and 'Silver Jubilee', no. 45666 *Cornwallis*, wisely sought a banker at Oxenholme in the form of Ivatt Class 4 2–6–0, no. 43029. The pair are seen at Lambrigg Crossing with the 8.50 a.m. Saturdays-only Blackpool Central–Glasgow train on 25 July 1964. *(Peter Fitton)*

A WD 2–8–0, no. 90419, hurries an Up freight passed the diminutive signal-box at Lambrigg Crossing on 25 July 1964. *(Peter Fitton)*

On reaching Grayrigg there is respite for a few miles before the final slog to Shap Summit. Passing the wayside station at Grayrigg is 'Princess Coronation', no. 46240 *City of Coventry* at the head of the northbound 'Royal Scot' on 7 May 1955. While passenger services had been withdrawn the previous years, goods facilities were retained here until 1960. *(M.N. Bland, www.transporttreasury.co.uk)*

In the opposite direction 'Princess Coronation', no. 46241 *City of Edinburgh*, hurries passed Grayrigg signal-box with the 9 a.m. Perth–Euston on 25 July 1964. The Howgill Fells loom ominously in the background. *(Peter Fitton)*

A last view of Grayrigg sees Stanier Class 5 4–6–0, no. 45024, piloting a 'Princess Coronation', no. 46224 *Princess Alexandra*, on a parcels train on 13 July 1963. It was unusual to see a double-headed combination featuring one of these Pacifics but it appears to be leaking steam at the front end which may be the reason for the assistance. *(Peter Fitton)*

A Class 87, no. 87032 *Kenilworth*, with a southbound express leaves Low Gill behind on 13 August 1983. The M6 can be seen immediately above the rear of the train. The railway veers to the right before passing through the Lune Gorge which lies at the base of the Howgill Fells in the background. *(Tom Heavyside)*

A Class 50, no. 443, rounds the curve near Low Gill with a southbound express on 17 July 1971. The motorway is hidden behind the banking to the left while Fell Head stands guard at the southern end of the Lune Gorge. *(Tom Heavyside)*

At Low Gill the train comes face to face with the Howgill Fells before curving to the left to join the River Lune. Less than 30 miles from Lancaster, BR 'Britannia', no. 70053 *Moray Firth* heads the three-coach Keswick portion of the Lakes Express through the Lune Gorge on 26 July 1963. *(Peter Fitton)*

At about the same spot in the Lune Gorge we see 'Princess Coronation', no. 46254 *City of Stoke-on-Trent*, at the head of the Euston–Glasgow relief in the early evening of 1 August 1964. It is hard to believe that all but one of these magnificent locomotives would be gone in just six weeks. *(Peter Fitton)*

A classic view of the Lune Gorge sees Carlisle Kingmoor Class 5 4–6–0, no. 45323, on an Up freight in the late afternoon of 13 July 1963. *(Peter Fitton)*

A 'Silver Jubilee', no. 45613 *Kenya*, hurries a Glasgow–Manchester express comprising mainly LMS coaches over Dillicar Troughs at about 5.30 p.m. on 13 July 1963. At the far end of the valley lies Tebay. *(Peter Fitton)*

A final view of the Lune Gorge as 'Royal Scot', no. 46115 *Scots Guardsman*, heads the Manchester–Glasgow express over Dillicar Troughs on 25 July 1964. *(Peter Fitton)*

A 'Princess Coronation', no. 46248 *City of Leeds*, restarts its lightweight train from Tebay station on 15 August 1964. On the right are the lines that crossed the Pennines to Darlington. *(Peter Fitton)*

A coal train passes through Tebay station on its way north behind a Stanier Class 5 4–6–0, no. 44993, on 17 October 1967. The line to the right leads to Tebay shed, which survived until the final year of steam in 1968. *(Tom Heavyside)*

An overall view of Tebay and its motive power depot is partially obscured by the smokescreen created by the combination of locomotives in charge of a Blackpool Central–Glasgow relief on 15 August 1964, just weeks away from the closure of Blackpool Central. The engines are Fowler 2–6–4 tank, no. 42414, leading 'Silver Jubilee', no. 45598 *Basutoland*. The Pennine route to Darlington crosses to the left. *(Peter Fitton)*

Tebay to Carlisle

The climb to Shap begins in earnest at 1 in 75 beyond Tebay. In steam days the assistance of one of the banking locomotives at Tebay shed would often be required. About 3 miles beyond Tebay stood the lonely outpost known as Scout Green signal-box on the left, witness to so many slow moving expresses tackling the last few miles to the summit. Also on the left, a little further on, we pass Shap Wells Hotel, built in 1850 after it was discovered that the local water had beneficial properties.

Once the summit is reached at 916ft above sea level it is down hill all the way to Carlisle. Immediately beyond the summit is the granite works where quarrying is mainly for railway ballast, although granite setts were once produced for roads. The A6 trunk road joins the railway on the left while on our right is Shap Quarry where limestone is produced. Mention has already been made of Westmorland slates, used for tiling, and Shap granite, whose use as a building stone was in fact quite limited (the church at Tebay being one of the exceptions). One of the best-known building materials from these parts is the grey carboniferous limestone seen in many of the buildings north of Lancaster. Often however, because of severe weather conditions in this part of the world, a rendering of various types is placed over the original material to improve the resistance to wind and rain.

About 2 miles beyond the summit, the village of Shap can be seen on the left. A station building survives on the left, long after closure in 1968. A little further on, both the A6 and the M6 cross over to the left of the line and as they do so look out for a farmhouse situated close to the line on the left. This is Thrimby Grange, a farm that is noteworthy as a popular photographic spot of southbound trains climbing towards Shap. About 4 miles further on, beyond the site of the former station at Clifton and Lowther, the track-bed of the former NER route from Appleby and Kirkby Stephen may be seen down on the right before it joined the WCML at Eden Valley Junction. A cutting takes us under the A6 before emerging to cross over the M6 motorway. At this point look to the right for a good view of the surviving feature of Clifton Hall – its pele tower dating from about 1500. Such towers were used as places of refuge during border raids and are mainly found in Cumbria and Northumberland. After crossing the River Lowther and then beyond two cuttings, look left for a view of Yanwath Hall, complete with fourteenth-century pele tower and battlements raised at the corner.

As we cross the River Eamont look left, down the river, for a view of Helvellyn, one of the highest peaks in the Lake District at 3,118ft. It is visible mainly because Ullswater lies directly in its path giving a comparatively unimpeded view. Crossing the A66 trunk road that runs from the west to the east of the country the line now curves sharply to the right to Penrith South Junction where, on an embankment to the left, the former Cockermouth, Keswick and Penrith Railway converged with the WCML. The picturesque route was one of many lines to disappear in the aftermath of the Beeching Report. Passing over the M6 once again we now enter Penrith, a red sandstone market town. The underlying rock structure of Triassic sandstones is the same as that encountered in parts of the Midlands, Cheshire and Lancashire.

Behind the station stands Penrith Castle on the right, completed in the fourteenth century for Bishop Strickland, but added to by Richard, Duke of Gloucester (later Richard III), while in residence. By 1550 the castle had become a ruin and it has changed little since then. Beyond the station the train curves left to the north of the town. The hill on the right is Penrith Beacon, 937ft high, and used in the past for warning of national emergencies. The last serious occasion on which it was used was at the time of the 1745 Rising. The 'pike' upon the hill was built in 1719 and is partially hidden among the trees these days.

Between Penrith and Carlisle there were intermediate stations at Plumpton, Calthwaite, Southwaite and Wreay. All of them lost their passenger services between 1943 and 1952 although station buildings survive at Southwaite on the right and Wreay on the left.

The last of the lineside apparatus for exchanging mail at speed with Travelling Post Office trains was situated to the north of Penrith. The last exchange took place on 4 October 1971 after 133 years of service.

From both the south and the north side of Penrith it is possible to see, on the right, Cross Fell, which at 2,930ft is the highest mountain in the Pennines. It is less than 15 miles from the railway. Several rounded hills can be seen on the right over the next few miles. These were formed by glacial action. Old valleys were broadened and deepened by the movement of the glaciers .and when the ice melted large mounds of boulder clay were left to form elongated ridges. These are known as drumlins.

We are now approaching Carlisle, the principal town in Cumbria. Across to the right, at Upperby New Junction, was Carlisle Upperby motive power depot, home to many of the most powerful LMS locomotives in the heyday of steam. The building can still be seen. After crossing the avoiding lines we are joined on the left by the line from Workington (Cumbria Coast line) and on the right by the lines from Leeds (former MR) and Newcastle (NER). Carlisle station was completed in 1848 in a Tudor Gothic style. This is the most northerly extent of the LNWR system and for Glasgow, Edinburgh and Perth, the journey continues along the former Caledonian Railway system.

Shortly after leaving Tebay, the steep climb resumes with 5 miles at 1 in 75 for most of the way to Shap Summit. On a wet and windy day, 'Princess Coronation', no. 46241 *City of Edinburgh*, hauls a motley collection of coaches, vans and trucks away from Tebay in the face of a westerly depression. The train is heading north at about 6.45 p.m. on 30 July 1964. *(Peter Fitton)*

The climb has begun in earnest and only days before the end of regular steam over Shap, a BR 'Britannia', no. 70024 (formerly named *Vulcan*), joins forces with its banking engine, BR Class 4 4–6–0, no. 75030, to create a magnificent display of smoke (and, presumably, rhythmic noise) at Greenholme with a northbound freight on 20 December 1967. *(Peter Fitton)*

Still climbing, further up the incline at Shap Wells, engine nos 70024 and 75030 continue the struggle towards the summit, ten days before the end of regular steam in the area. *(Peter Fitton)*

Later on the same day, 20 December 1967, another freight is seen ascending the incline at Shap Wells. On this occasion, Stanier class 8F 2–8–0, no. 48491, has spurned the use of a banker and is going for glory. Surely this sight of one of man's greatest creations fighting the elements is a fitting way to remember the era of steam over Shap. *(Peter Fitton)*

Scout Green is the location and 'Princess Coronation', no. 46241 *City of Edinburgh*, in charge of the 'Royal Scot' on 21 May 1958, has covered 3 miles of the incline since Tebay and now has less than 3 miles to go to the summit. It appears to be coping well although there seems to be interest on the footplate in the steam issuing from the cylinders. *(Gavin Morrison)*

A double-headed combination of locomotives is required to haul a massive seventeen-coach load up Shap on 26 May 1958. The train is the Manchester–Glasgow express and the locomotives making a splendid spectacle of themselves are Class 2P 4–4–0, no. 40694, and BR 'Britannia', no. 70054 *Dornoch Firth*. As the 4–4–0 appears to be a Preston engine, it is reasonable to conclude that additional coaches were added there. (*Gavin Morrison*)

In its final year of service, a 'Princess Royal', no. 46208 *Princess Helena Victoria*, is seen at Shap Wells under ominous clouds while on the approach to the summit on 4 August 1962. *(Peter Fitton)*

The 'Royal Scot' has begun its descent from the summit on its way south behind 'Princess Coronation', no. 46229 *Duchess of Hamilton*, on 26 May 1958. As with no. 6100 *Royal Scot* in 1933, no. 6229 *Duchess of Hamilton* (at that time streamlined) visited America. It assumed the identity of sister engine no. 6220 *Coronation* and, together with a new train of 'Coronation Scot' stock in 1939, covered 3,000 miles in a little over three weeks before being exhibited at the New York World's Fair. However, war had broken out while the train was still in New York, and it was not until 1943 that the locomotive returned to Britain where it assumed its original identity as no. 6229. *(Gavin Morrison)*

The summit is in sight and Stanier Class 5 4–6–0, no. 45072, with a Saturdays only Glasgow–Morecambe express, is coasting down the incline, past Shap Summit signal-box, on 22 July 1967. *(Peter Fitton)*

Another view of the 'Royal Scot', this time heading south passed Harrison's Sidings towards the summit with 'Princess Coronation', no. 46243 *City of Lancaster*, in charge on Saturday 29 August 1959. During that summer's timetable the train was booked non-stop except on Sundays. *(Gavin Morrison)*

A double-headed combination in LMS livery comprising Class 2P 4–4–0, no. 403, and 'Royal Scot' no. 6157 *The Royal Artilleryman* head south for Shap Summit on 27 August 1949 having just passed a northbound train. *(J.D. Darby)*

On its way to the summit, rebuilt 'Silver Jubilee', no. 45736 *Phoenix*, passes Shap Station with a Summer Saturday Glasgow–Blackpool Central express on 18 July 1964. The station's accessories such as the water tower, goods crane and livestock pen would all be swept away in this decade of rationalisation and the station would close in 1968. As for *Phoenix*, it survived a few more weeks before withdrawal with the only other rebuilt member of the class, *Comet*. *(Peter Fitton)*

It has been mainly uphill since Carlisle for 'Silver Jubilee', no. 45698 *Mars*, as it heads the 10.35 a.m. Glasgow–Liverpool Exchange express passed Thrimby Grange on 18 July 1959. No. 45698 was based at Liverpool's Bank Hall shed throughout the BR era. *(J.D. Darby)*

Having left Penrith behind on its journey south, 'Princess Coronation', no. 46231 *Duchess of Atholl* is seen with the 'Royal Scot' at Eden Valley Junction on 30 August 1958 as it tackles the gradient towards Shap Summit, still the best part of 10 miles away. This engine was based at Glasgow's Polmadie depot but, judging by the amount of coal in the tender, may have come on at Carlisle. *(Gavin Morrison)*

Penrith station is in sight as a Class 2 2–6–0, no. 46447, pulls away with a train for Workington in May 1950. These engines replaced the LNWR 'Cauliflower' 0–6–0s on duties such as this and no. 46447 has since been acquired for preservation. *(R.F. Roberts courtesy of the Stephenson Locomotive Society)*

Refreshments are waiting to be carried aboard as BR 'Britannia', no. 70039 *Sir Christopher Wren* from Kingmoor depot, arrives at Penrith's platform 1 from the north. Note the Wymans newspaper kiosk, once a common sight, on platform 2. *(David Lawrence/Photos from The Fifties)*

An ex-LNWR 2F 0–6–0, no. 58376, runs passed light engine north of Penrith in May 1951. These locomotives known as 'Cauliflowers' were found in many ex-LNWR sheds between the Midlands and Carlisle. The last examples of this class were withdrawn at the beginning of 1956 having been replaced on many duties by the LMS and BR 2–6–0s such as no. 46447 seen at Penrith. (*F. & R. Hewitt courtesy of the Stephenson Locomotive Society*)

A Stanier Class 5 4–6–0, no. 45369, pilots a 'Silver Jubilee', no. 45732 *Sanspareil*, at Wreay on the journey south from Carlisle with a Glasgow-Birmingham express in May 1951. The 'Silver Jubilee' was one of several of its class, including *Phoenix* seen at Shap, named after early Liverpool and Manchester locomotives. (*F. & R. Hewitt courtesy of the Stephenson Locomotive Society*)

This view of Carlisle from the south sees 'Princess Coronation', no. 46225 *Duchess of Gloucester*, accelerate away from the Border City with the Up 'Mid-Day Scot', running about 12 minutes late on 3 September 1955. The tracks on the right are crossing over the lines from Newcastle and from the Settle and Carlisle route, both of which join the West Coast Main Line on the approach to the station. Joining the main line from the left is the Cumbrian Coast route, while passing underneath the train are the avoiding lines used by freight and for locomotives gaining access to the former North British Railway depot at Carlisle Canal. *(Brian Connell/Photos from The Fifties)*

Carlisle Upperby motive power depot was one of the principal sheds on the West Coast Main Line and, from time to time, housed examples of all the largest classes of express locomotives. In this overview of the shed yard we see the pioneer 'Princess Royal', no. 46200 *The Princess Royal* in maroon livery at the buffer stops. It had been withdrawn two years earlier with its remaining sisters but was stored pending a bid to preserve it. This did not succeed but two other members of the class, nos 46201 and 46203, did manage to survive the cutter's torch. Closest to the camera is BR Class 9 2–10–0, no. 92006, with 'Jinty' 0–6–0, no. 47295, and Class 2 2–6–0, no. 46426. In the distance to the right is an unidentified rebuilt 'Patriot' while beyond 'The Princess Royal' are the partly hidden 'Royal Scot', no. 46110 (formerly *Grenadier Guardsman*), and rebuilt 'Patriot', no. 45512 *Bunsen*. An Ivatt Class 4 2–6–0 can also be seen in this view dating from 30 August 1964. The shed can still be seen today from the train. *(Hugh Ballantyne)*

'The Royal Scot' arrives at the Border City on 9 August 1960. There is a deafening noise from 'Princess Coronation', no. 46221 *Queen Elizabeth*, as the safety valves are lifted by jets of steam. The fireman monitors progress as the Camden-based locomotive's tender is replenished with water prior to departure suggesting that it will work through to Glasgow. *(Gavin Morrison)*

Before the Grouping of the various railway companies into just four operators in 1923, Carlisle Citadel station, like Joseph, must have displayed many colours because no less than seven companies, each with their own locomotive and coaching stock liveries, used the station. No other station in the country could compare. The London & North Western Railway, the Midland Railway, the Caledonian Railway, the Glasgow and South Western Railway and the Maryport and Carlisle Railway were to be subsumed into the new LMS while the North British Railway and North Eastern Railway would become part of the LNER. Even in BR days there was variety, and there was always a chance to see an Eastern Region locomotive such as a B1 4–6–0 on a Newcastle train. No. 61217 of Carlisle Canal depot awaits departure from the south end of Carlisle with the 2 p.m. to Newcastle on 7 May 1959. *(John Hilton)*

A regular sight at the south end of the station was of a Pacific waiting to take over the 'Royal Scot'. As the
Up 'Thames Clyde Express' from Glasgow St Enoch to London St Pancras was usually scheduled to arrive
a little later, there was often the chance to see two locomotives waiting to take over their successive trains.
In October 1952 'Princess Coronation', no. 46239 *City of Chester* waits to take over the 'Royal Scot' while a
Leeds-based 'Silver Jubilee', no. 45605 *Cyprus*, stands alongside for the arrival of the 'Thames Clyde
Express'. In actual fact, the 'Jubilee' would pilot the train engine, 'Royal Scot', no. 46109 *Royal Engineers*, to
Leeds. (*R. Butterfield/Initial Photographics*)

A view of the north end of Carlisle Citadel station as Leeds-based 'Royal Scot', no. 46117 *Welsh Guardsman*, in fine fettle, arrives with 'The Thames–Clyde Express' on 23 August 1952. (*J. Robertson, www.transporttreasury.co.uk*)

Another arrival at the south end of Carlisle station is 'Princess Royal', no. 46210 *Lady Patricia*, with 'The Mid-Day Scot' on 2 October 1954. It is interesting to compare the water column on the platform with the water tower as seen at Shap station. *(T. Noble, D. Chatfield Collection)*

A change of locomotives at Carlisle's north end sees 'Royal Scot', no. 46141 *The North Staffordshire Regiment*, after coming off the Manchester–Glasgow express, and another 'Royal Scot', no. 46144 *Honourable Artillery Company*, attaching to the train for the remainder of the journey to Glasgow Central on 24 July 1963. *(Peter Fitton)*

By the time of this view of the 'Thames–Clyde Express' at Carlisle, ex-LNER A3 Pacifics, drafted into Leeds Holbeck to replace the 'Royal Scots', were in regular use on the train. Here we see no. 60082 *Neil Gow* after arrival from Leeds. The shed code for Leeds at this time was 55A whereas in older views it was 20A (changed 1957). The date is 20 August 1960. *(Gavin Morrison)*

A final view of Carlisle station shows a BR 'Clan', no. 72006 *Clan Mackenzie*, leaving with the 1.05 p.m. Manchester–Glasgow while 'Princess Coronation', no. 46249 *City of Sheffield* waits its turn to take over the Sunday Down 'Royal Scot' from Euston on 30 June 1963. *(Hugh Ballantyne)*

'The Royal Scot' approaches Carlisle from the north behind one of Glasgow's 'Princess Coronation' Pacifics, no. 46230 *Duchess of Buccleuch*, on 23 August 1952. *(J. Robertson, www.transporttreasury.co.uk)*

Carlisle to Beattock

The modern traveller is left with no obvious clue as to the significance of Carlisle as a railway centre in the days before the Grouping of 1923. Until then the trains of six railway companies used the station known as Carlisle Citadel; the LNWR, the Midland Railway and North Eastern Railway from the south-east, the Maryport & Carlisle Railway from the south-west, and the Caledonian Railway and North British Railway from the north. The Glasgow and South Western Railway's trains also had running powers into the city. The different liveries of these railway companies must have made a cheerful sight indeed in those days. Much of the original station remains as designed by Sir William Tite.

Immediately on leaving the station a view of the citadel can be seen on the right. It was built in 1543 to guard the approach to the city but rebuilt in 1821 to a design by Sir Robert Smirke to house the Assize Court. The old city walls, or what remains of them, lie close to the railway, the west walls being visible above on the right. Behind the walls are the Cathedral and Priory of St Mary. The cathedral was built in the twelfth century when Henry I granted the site for founding a religious establishment. The building, which is mainly of red sandstone, was restored in the nineteenth century. Passing under the inner ring road we see the castle on the right. Begun in the eleventh century it was rebuilt many times following invasion by the Scots.

Beyond the River Caldew we cross the course of Hadrian's Wall, of which nothing survives in Carlisle. Having crossed the River Eden we pass, on the right, the wooded site of Kingmoor, another of the principal locomotive depots on the WCML. Built by the Caledonian Railway it was home to all of the main express types in its later years and the last survivors of the 'Scots', 'Patriots' and 'Clans' were based here. It closed at the beginning of 1968. In contrast, on the left, is the modern traction depot before the marshalling yards. This is the first motive power depot since leaving Crewe whereas in steam days there would have been nine, excluding Lostock Hall and Green Ayre which were off the main line. Passing under the former Waverley route to Edinburgh we encounter what remains of the marshalling yards on the left. Beyond the sidings, on the left, is the village of Rockcliffe. Its former station lay in the vicinity of the flyover, used for freight traffic.

About 2 miles further on, the site of Floriston station is located by one of the few level crossings on the WCML, while the water troughs lay a little to the north. Like Rockcliffe and Gretna stations, Floriston closed in the 1950s. Beyond the broad River Esk we pass under the A74 trunk road to Glasgow. The remains of a former NBR branch join the WCML on the right just beyond the road bridge, and then after another road bridge we pass the site of Gretna station and cross the modest River Sark into Scotland.

The former GSWR route to Glasgow, Kilmarnock, Ayr and Stanraer branches off to the left while we continue along the former Caledonian Railway main line to Glasgow, with Gretna Green over to the left. Beyond a cutting the line curves to the left on an embankment and this rural location, before the next cutting, was the scene of the worst railway accident in Britain in 1915. 227 people died, mostly troops from the Royal Scot regiment bound for the Dardanelles. Signalling errors were the cause of the accident and, on the right, a white name board bearing the name Quintinshill marks the location.

Beyond the A74 trunk road that crosses over to our right we pass Kirkpatrick-Fleming and the site of its station. Kirtle Water meanders to the left of the railway as a series of cuttings takes us to Kirtlebridge. Look out on the left for the sixteenth-century towers of Robgill and Bonshaw. The former is now part of a modern mansion while Bonshaw Tower was considered to be a place of some strength in the sixteenth century and has long been the seat of the Irvine family, a small border clan. These houses were peculiarly Scottish although bearing some resemblance to the pele towers of Northern England. On crossing Kirtle Water the village of Kirtlebridge can be seen. Its station, like all those between Gretna and Beattock with the exception of Lockerbie, closed in 1960. As the line curves to the right it is possible to see the track-bed of the former Caledonian branch line to Annan on the left. Under the A74 and emerging onto an embankment we cross Mein Water, at which point look 200yds to the right, by the side of the river, for the earthwork remains of the Roman fort of Blatobulgium, occupied between 80 and 180AD. As the line curves towards the left a conspicuous flat-topped hill may be seen ahead on the right-hand side. This is Burnswark on which was situated another Roman fort. It is visible from the train for several miles. There are, in fact, the earthworks of a number of Roman sites along the route, which is an ancient one adopted by both the road and the railway.

Ecclefechan, a town of red sandstone buildings and without its station, is visible briefly on the left. The church contains the grave of Thomas Carlyle, the historian and writer, who was born here in 1795. Beyond the long cuttings, the railway crosses a river known as the Water of Milk on the approach to Lockerbie, an Annandale market town, and the only populated area between Carlisle and Carstairs (a distance of over 73 miles) to be served by a station. The town grew up around a sixteenth-century Johnstone tower and has been the scene of savage fighting between the Maxwells and Johnstones. The Maxwells held the lower end of Annandale and the Johnstones the central part. In 1593 at Dryfe Sands, to the west of Lockerbie, the Johnstones defeated the Maxwells, who lost 700 men in the last of the great border feuds. Surprisingly, this was the heaviest clan battle in Scotland's history in terms of casualties. Beyond the village we cross Dryfe Water, a tributary of the River Annan.

After Lockerbie we pass the sites of former stations at Nethercleugh, Dinwoodie and Wamphray. Beyond the last of these stations we cross the River Annan. The A74 trunk road crosses over the railway on the approach to Beattock. The station closed in 1972 and the site of the former motive power depot may be seen on the left. Its allocation of steam locomotives included the bankers required to help trains climb to Beattock Summit, 10 miles further north. The track-bed of the former branch line to Moffat lies to the right. Moffat is a small spa town that has associations with Robert Burns and is also one of the gateways to the countryside of Sir Walter Scott to the east. Joseph Locke, who built much of the WCML, is buried here and so is John Macadam, who made a great contribution to the quality of the roads.

The river on our right is Evan Water, the main tributary of the River Annan. It follows the same course as the road and for much of the climb to Beattock summit. During the course of the climb we pass from the region of Dumfries and Galloway into Strathclyde. Since Beattock the climb has stiffened to between 1 in 69 and 1 in 88, a gradient that is unrelenting all the way to the summit, marked by a sign on the right. From now on, apart from the odd uphill stretch, it is downhill all the way to Glasgow.

In this look back at Carlisle, Stanier Class 5 4–6–0, no. 45295, at Etterby Junction, crosses the River Eden and forges north with a parcels train on 4 September 1963. *(Peter Fitton)*

Beyond the river, on the east side of the railway, stood Carlisle's other major motive power depot at Kingmoor. In this view we see Kingmoor-based 'Princess Royal', no. 46203 *Princess Margaret Rose* in green livery, being turned on 29 August 1962 prior to working a Euston–Perth express from Carlisle. This locomotive is believed to have achieved the highest speed for its class at 102.5mph and at the time of this picture was less than two months away from withdrawal. Luckily, it survives today in preservation. Incidentally, the gentleman crossing the West Coast Main Line beyond the tender of no. 46203 is none other than famous railway photographer, Eric Treacy, later Bishop of Wakefield. *(Peter Fitton)*

Kingmoor depot is clearly seen in the background as 'Princess Coronation', no. 46232 *Duchess of Montrose* restarts a seventeen-coach down 'Royal Scot', having reversed for wrong line working on Sunday 14 August 1960. The driver is leaning well out of his cab to see what is happening towards the front end of the locomotive. The bridge above the second coach carries the Waverley route to Edinburgh. *(Gavin Morrison)*

Along what was formerly the route of the Caledonian Railway, 'Princess Coronation', no. 46232 *Duchess of Montrose*, is seen at Rockcliffe, about 4 miles north of Carlisle with the northbound 'Royal Scot' on 17 April 1954. Note how the running-plate on these non-streamlined engines continues down to the buffers. *(Gavin Morrison)*

We have just crossed the River Sark, which marks the Scottish border, and here at Gretna Junction, a 'Princess 'Coronation', no. 46246 *City of Manchester*, is about to leave Scotland with 'The Royal Scot' on 4 June 1960. This junction marks the point where the former Glasgow and South Western Railway territory began and its main line for Dumfries, Kilmarnock and Glasgow is seen veering away to the left. Less than 2 miles further north on the Caledonian route is Quintinshill, scene of Britain's worst railway accident in 1915. *(Gavin Morrison)*

Kirkpatrick is about 4 miles north of Gretna Junction and passing through on a Glasgow–London Euston summer extra is 'Princess Coronation', no. 46234 *Duchess of Abercorn* on 4 June 1960. Kirkpatrick station closed in the same year. *(Gavin Morrison)*

Kirtlebridge is a further 4 miles beyond Kirkpatrick and in this picture, also taken on 4 June 1960, a BR 'Clan', no. 72008 *Clan Macleod*, is seen at the head of the Perth–Euston express. It appears as if there were sidings once on the left while over to the right the station sidings and goods dock, complete with crane, appear to be out of use. In fact, Kirtlebridge closed in the year that this picture was taken. *(Gavin Morrison)*

Lockerbie is over 25 miles from Carlisle and the first town of any size. Appearing to be working wrong line at the station is BR Class 4 2–6–0, no.76113, alongside the Down platform. Note the water column at the end of the up platform. At the time of writing, this station is the only one that is open between Carlisle and Carstairs, a distance of almost 74 miles. (*Norris Forrest, www.transporttreasury.co.uk*)

A Carlisle Kingmoor class 5 4–6–0, no. 44900, passes Beattock station on 20 May 1961 at the head of a Down express without calling for a banker. The engine and its nine coaches will now tackle the next ten miles at gradients of between 1 in 69 and 1 in 88, some of the steepest gradients anywhere on Britain's main lines. The reporting number seems to have been applied in a hurry as it is upside-down! The motive power depot on the right had an allocation of tank engines that were used for banking trains up to the summit. An LMS 2–6–4 tank engine can just be seen in the shed yard in the distance. Beattock station closed in 1972. (*Gavin Morrison*)

About 5 miles beyond Beattock station and more than half way to the summit, 'Princess Coronation', no. 46255 *City of Hereford* appears to make light work of the five-coach 9.25 a.m. Crewe–Perth as it climbs passed Greskine Box to Beattock Summit on 9 October 1963. This train was a regular working for the 'Princess Coronation' class in their final years. In the background is the A74 trunk road. *(Hugh Ballantyne)*

A Stanier Class 5 4–6–0, no. 45176, of Motherwell shed, emerges from the cutting north of Greskine Box with a Down mineral train on 31 May 1966. It is banked by a Fairburn 2–6–4 tank engine, no. 42694, hidden behind the brake van. *(Hugh Ballantyne)*

No peace for the residents of the surrounding woodland as 'Princess Royal', no. 46209 *Princess Beatrice*, storms Beattock Bank with a Birmingham–Glasgow express on 4 September 1950. *(J.D. Darby)*

The Down 'Royal Scot' is seen at Harthope on the upper stages of the climb to Beattock summit on 4 June 1960 behind 'Princess Coronation', no. 46247 *City of Liverpool*. At this time the train was reduced to eight coaches but given a faster timing of 7 hours 15 minutes with a departure from Euston at 9.05 a.m. *(Gavin Morrison)*

Beattock Summit is reached by BR 'Clan', no. 72000 *Clan Buchanan*, with an Up express on 14 July 1962, a few months before the locomotive was withdrawn from service at the age of about ten years. (*Gavin Morrison*)

Beattock to Glasgow

Beyond Beattock Summit and immediately after the A74 crosses to the right over the line, note the stream below on our left. It is Clydes Burn, a tributary of the River Clyde which we soon cross on the approach to Elvanfoot, approached via a right-hand curve. This village was a favourite stopping place of Robert Burns on his journey between Edinburgh and his home in Dumfries. The former Caledonian Railway branch line from Wanlockhead joined the main line from the left but it closed many years ago. It was once the highest railway line in the British Isles. The former station lay to the south of the village at the junction with the former branch line.

Through the cuttings north of Elvanfoot we part company with the A74 until the outskirts of Glasgow. The railway is obliged to find the easier gradient nearer to the river. Approaching Crawford look out on the right for the formation of a railway line that was used in the construction of the Camps Reservoir, about 3 miles up the valley to the east. Crawford station was situated just before the meandering Clyde presses against the line on the right-hand side. At this point, look out to the right, to a copse across the river, for a glimpse of Tower Lindsay, part of an old castle that was the seat of the Lindsays, known as the Earls of Crawford from the twelfth century to 1488. It then passed to the Douglas family and at one time was briefly held by James V of Scotland, who used it as one of his hunting seats. The tower is seen more easily in winter.

Having crossed the Clyde the railway curves to the right as it approaches Abington, whose station, like all others between Beattock and Carstairs, was closed in 1965, a product of the Beeching era. Just south of the village of Lamington, similarly without a station, the Clyde crosses to our right. High above us and to the left is the notable conical landmark, Tinto, 2,335ft high and smoothed into its present shape by glacial action. From the mountain it is possible to see both east and west coasts of Scotland and even Ireland on a clear day.

A series of cuttings takes us to Symington where trains with portions for Glasgow and Edinburgh, including the 'Royal Scot', used to split instead of at Carstairs. Symington was once a railway junction with the former Caledonian line to Peebles on the right. The site of the station lies just beyond the A72 trunk road over which the railway crosses. Thankerton, at the foot of the conical Quothquan Hill on the right, is another village that lost its station.

On the approach to Carstairs we cross the River Clyde once more. The Strawfranks water troughs were situated over a mile south of the station. They were the last troughs along the route. The line veering away to the right on our approach to the station is the Edinburgh route. The former locomotive depot was situated to the right of the station and closed in 1966. About 2 miles beyond Carstairs station, the railway is joined on the left by the branch line from Lanark just before the river crossing. A little further, beyond the level crossing, is the site of Cleghorn station. Braidwood too, has lost its station but Carluke is still served by the railway. Another 2 miles on, Law Junction once boasted large marshalling yards but the station closed in 1965 and, with the decline of coal, iron and steel, little remains apart from the junction where a line branches off to Wishaw Central station. Wishaw is served by Glasgow–Lanark suburban services, which rejoin the main line on the right about 2 miles south of Motherwell, but its station at Wishaw South closed in 1958. Likewise, Flemington station has long since disappeared but Shieldmuir is one of a handful of new stations to open in the post-electrification era.

Motherwell was transformed by coal and iron, and yet the nineteenth-century traveller and writer, William Cobbett, wrote that if he were to live in Scotland, Motherwell would be the place he would choose. This was just twenty years before the Lanarkshire coalfield was developed. Today, all has changed again. The massive Ravenscraig steelworks that was situated on the right has disappeared although the Dalzell ironworks remains at the time of writing. Leaving Motherwell station the line that joins us from the left is a suburban loop line which takes in Hamilton and rejoins the WCML a few miles nearer to Glasgow. Almost opposite, on the right, the line branching away at Lesmahagow Junction leads to Mossend Yard, Coatbridge and Stirling. The former motive power depot at Motherwell was situated in the fork of the two lines and is still a base for diesels. After crossing the South Calder Water we skirt round the side of Strathclyde Country Park on the left with Strathclyde Loch in the centre of the park. Completed in 1976 it covers an area that was formerly blighted by coal workings. About 3 miles north-west of Motherwell the WCML is joined by the former Caledonian main line (now a secondary route) from Edinburgh on the right, shortly after passing the site of the former Fallside station. The line curves to the left under the M74, through Uddingston station and across the Clyde.

On emerging from the next cutting we are joined again by the Hamilton loop line on the left as we approach Newton station. A little further, a suburban line diverges in the next cutting to Glasgow via Cathcart. The line now passes through the industrial suburb of Cambuslang, served by a local station, and a mile further on is joined by the Caledonian lines from Coatbridge and Airdrie as we approach Rutherglen, a royal borough since the twelfth century. On the right at Rutherglen, lines once connected to the east and north sides of Glasgow via a triangular junction. Further out to the right the Glasgow Celtic football stadium can be seen at Parkhead. Once through the station and short cutting we approach Polmadie. The carriage sidings on the right occupy the site of what was Polmadie motive power depot, once the principal Scottish loco depot for the WCML. Careful observers may spot Hampden Park football stadium on the left.

The line curves sharply to the right joining lines from the southern suburbs and from Kilmarnock before joining the coastal lines. On the right is the suburb known as the Gorbals as we cross the A74 trunk road and then the Clyde for the last time. Glasgow Bridge (also known as Jamaica Bridge from the days when Glasgow was a major port for the West India trade) can be seen on the right, and beyond that, a suspension bridge. Also visible on the right beyond the suspension bridge is St Andrews Roman Catholic Cathedral in the gothic style and the Merchants' Steeple, completed in 1665. Finally we enter Glasgow Central station – spacious and retaining much of its Victorian splendour.

On the climb to Beattock Summit from the north another 'Princess Coronation', no. 46251 *City of Nottingham,* has just crossed the Clyde near Crawford with a returning Glasgow to Nottingham special composed of LMS stock on 5 October 1963. *(Hugh Ballantyne)*

The peace and quiet of Elvanfoot station is aroused by the appearance of BR 'Britannia', no. 70045, on an express. The locomotive's nameplates have been removed. It was formerly *Lord Rowallan*. Elvanfoot station closed in 1965. *(Norris Forrest, www.transporttreasury.co.uk)*

The next stop is Beattock for the 9.25 a.m. Sundays Glasgow–Birmingham (with coaches from Edinburgh), seen hurrying through Elvanfoot on 30 June 1957 with 'Princess Coronation', no. 46225 *Duchess of Gloucester* at the front end. *(Ron Gee)*

The unusual juxtaposition of these locomotives at Crawford station can be explained by the ex-Caledonian Railway class 3P 4–4–0, no. 54505, having given assistance to the overnight sleeper from London. Following wrong line working, the sleeping car train engine, 'Princess Royal', no. 46200 *The Princess Royal*, resumed its journey to Glasgow in September 1953. *(M. Bolton, www.transporttreasury.co.uk)*

Shortly after passing the summit at Beattock the northbound travellers catch their first glimpse of the River Clyde, a mere burn near to its source. The river accompanies the railway closely for over ten miles and is seen being crossed by a 'Silver Jubilee', no. 45563 *Australia*, approaching the curve towards Crawford from the north. Note the diagonal line on the cabside, barring the locomotive from working south of Crewe due to tight clearances under the electric wires. *(Norris Forrest, www.transporttreasury.co.uk)*

The railway curves around Castle Hill before passing Abington, where BR 'Britannia', no. 70018, with nameplates removed (formerly *Flying Dutchman*), restarts a northbound service. The holes that can be seen clearly in the smoke deflectors were left when the handrails were removed following a serious accident, judged to have been caused by the presence of the handrails. *(Norris Forrest, www.transporttreasury.co.uk)*

Symington station is where the 'Royal Scot' used to be split, allowing separate coaches to be conveyed to Glasgow and Edinburgh. In LMS days we see 'Princess Royal' no. 6204 *Princess Louise* about to restart its train. (*J.T. Rutherford, www.transporttreasury.co.uk*)

More water is taken by 'Princess Coronation', no. 46222 *Queen Mary*, as it speeds over Strawfrank Troughs, the last water troughs on the journey to Glasgow. The train will shortly cross over the Clyde, in the distance to the left, before the approach to Carstairs. (*J. Robertson, www.transporttreasury.co.uk*)

Carstairs station sees the arrival of another northbound express with a 'Clan' 4–6–2, no. 72000 *Clan Buchanan*, at the head of the train. *(Alec Swain, www.transporttreasury.co.uk)*

An ex-Caledonian Railway 0–4–4 tank, no. 55124, is seen at Carstairs station on special duties, in charge of the 'Pentland–Tinto Express', an enthusiasts' outing. In the distance, between the locomotive and its coaches, stands the motive power depot at Carstairs. On the left is a Fairburn 2–6–4 tank engine and one of the variants of diesel multiple units which, though not seen before on this particular journey, have been commonplace in most parts of the country from the mid-1950s. *(Norris Forrest, www.transporttreasury.co.uk)*

'The Royal Scot' is seen passing through Motherwell on the last leg of its journey to Glasgow behind 'Princess Coronation', no. 46220 *Coronation*, in ex-works condition on 6 June 1953, four days after the coronation of Queen Elizabeth II. This explains the reason for the magnificent condition of this particular engine and its extra adornment at the front end. *(J. Robertson, www.transporttreasury.co.uk)*

An ex-Caledonian Railway 0–6–0, no. 57630, ambles through Motherwell with what appear to be coal empties. The train consists of wooden-bodied vehicles. The locomotive was based at nearby Hamilton at the time. *(Alec Swain, www.transporttreasury.co.uk)*

The Royal Burgh of Rutherglen is noted for its historical connections and its manufacturing, particularly chemicals and paper. Here it shows its industrial side as an ex-works 'Princess Coronation', no. 46231 *Duchess of Atholl*, hurries through on a summery 28 May 1955 with the 'Royal Scot'. The date is significant as it marked the beginning of a damaging seventeen-day ASLEF strike, bringing the railways to a standstill. Note the wooden-bodied trucks in the sidings to the right. (*J. Robertson, www.transporttreasury.co.uk*)

A Fairburn 2–6–4 tank, no. 42187, waits for business at Rutherglen station in this view looking towards Glasgow. The sidings are occupied by wagons and coaching stock. The footbridge over the rear of the train links the visible platforms with those over the main line. (*Rex Conway*)

About a mile beyond Rutherglen we reach Polmadie where an immaculate 'Princess Coronation', no. 46221 *Queen Elizabeth*, storms past at the head of the 'Royal Scot' on 9 May 1953, receiving an admiring look from the crew of Stanier Class 5 4–6–0, no.44786. (*J. Robertson, www.transporttreasury.co.uk*)

Polmadie shed, code 66A, was Glasgow's motive power depot for the principal West Coast Main Line locomotives and was situated less than 3 miles from the terminus. In this view we see visiting 'Princess Coronation', no. 46225 *Duchess of Gloucester*, in blue livery, complete with the 'Mid-Day Scot' headboard on 9 May 1953. In the background is Stanier Class 5 4–6–0, no.44787. (*J. Robertson, www.transporttreasury.co.uk*)

A Stanier Class 5 4–6–0, no. 45121, and an unidentified 'Silver Jubilee' gather pace as they forge past Eglinton Street with an up express. (*George Heiron, www.transporttreasury.co.uk*)

An ex-Caledonian Railway 0–4–4 tank, no. 55219, is seen at Eglinton Street with empty coaching stock. (*Rex Conway*)

Journey's end for the 'Royal Scot', seen crossing the Clyde for the last time as it enters Glasgow Central station behind 'Princess Coronation' no. 46231 *Duchess of Atholl* in April 1955. The original Clyde Bridge, with five lattice-girders and decorative iron arches, was removed in 1961 during resignalling and track alterations. *(Gavin Morrison)*

A view of platforms 5 to 9 at Glasgow Central where different generations of tank engines are seen in charge of local passenger trains and empty stock workings. BR Class 4 2–6–4 tank, no. 80056, is seen on the left while ex-Caledonian Railway 0–4–4 tank, no. 55237, stands at platform 5 on 12 September 1955. *(H.C. Casserley)*

Old and new motive power are represented here by a diesel multiple unit bound for Lanark and a Polmadie 'Royal Scot', no. 46105 *Cameron Highlander*, at platform 2 with an express for the south. *(George Heiron, www.transporttreasury.co.uk)*

Amid the vast expanse of Glasgow Central station, a 'Princess Coronation', no. 46224 *Princess Alexandra*, prepares to leave with the 'Royal Scot', taking us back to London Euston. *(P. Chancellor Collection)*

Diversions

Although the scheduled journey of the 'Royal Scot' is well known to many railway enthusiasts, the train itself has traversed many routes away from the WCML as a result of diversions. Engineering works have been the primary cause of the diversions, but weather-related problems such as flooding and the occasional accident or mishap have also caused the train to wander away from its traditional route.

A major disaster such as that at Harrow & Wealdstone in 1952 caused major disruption and WCML trains were required to use Paddington as well as St Pancras. A collision at Watford also caused the train to be diverted into St Pancras station. During the 'Big Freeze' in February 1963 the 'Royal Scot' was forced to take an even wider berth, using the ECML to King's Cross.

In the Midlands, the Northampton route has been a regular alternative route on Sundays and at other times when the WCML has been occupied in the area. Diversions away from the Trent Valley line, north of Rugby, have usually involved the train being routed via Perry Barr and Bushbury, avoiding Birmingham New Street and Wolverhampton High Level. A little further north, an accident between Crewe and Stafford necessitated diversions via Wellington and Shrewsbury, and even via Stoke, where 'Princess Coronations' were normally banned.

A derailment at Winsford in 1956 required a diversion to Chester and then Frodsham in order to regain the WCML at Acton Grange. Pacifics were used on this route. However, a landslip at Weaver Junction in the same year caused the train to take a circuitous route into Yorkshire via Normanton on the Midland route south of Leeds and then along the Settle & Carlisle line to the border. On many occasions the 'Royal Scot' has been routed around Manchester, usually following the former LNWR line through Stockport and then via Castlefield Junction to Eccles and Tyldesley, before rejoining the WCML at Wigan.

As described already, the 'Royal Scot' is no stranger to the Settle & Carlisle route but during engineering works between Garstang and Carnforth in 1959, while many trains were diverted via the Settle & Carlisle, the 'Royal Scot' was routed from Wigan through Chorley, Blackburn, Hellifield and then through Ingleton to Low Gill on the WCML south of Tebay. In 1971/2 and 1972/3 the train was diverted via the Settle & Carlisle on Sundays with Blackburn becoming a regular stop.

In the Midlands and the north of England there were several choices of routes available to take diverted traffic but in Scotland only the G&SWR route to Glasgow via Dumfries and Kilmarnock provided a reasonable alternative to the main line. At the northern end of the route, Glasgow St Enoch and Buchanan Street have both been used by this train instead of Central station.

Engineering works on the Trent Valley line causes the 'Royal Scot' to be diverted along the main line towards Birmingham. On Sunday 7 September 1958 'Princess Coronation' Pacific, no. 46250 *City of Lichfield*, passes over Holbrook Park troughs with the Down express. Rugby can be seen in the background. *(Michael Mensing)*

The 'Royal Scot' behind English Electric Type 4 1Co-Co1, no. D288, is seen further north, approaching Sandbach on the Manchester–Crewe route on Sunday 5 March 1961. It was diverted via this route because the WCML was closed north of Acton Bridge for works prior to the commencement of electric services on the line from Liverpool. *(Michael Mensing)*

A rebuilt 'Patriot', no. 45512 *Bunsen*, is in charge of the Down 'Royal Scot' as it negotiates Castlefield Junction on 8 May 1960. The locomotive was based at Carlisle Upperby at the time and will almost certainly work the train to Carlisle. Using the through platforms of London Road (soon to become Piccadilly), the train has passed Oxford Road and Knott Mill & Deansgate stations and is now taking the short line to the old Liverpool & Manchester route. From there it is likely that it would have travelled via Tyldesley and regained the WCML near Springs Branch, Wigan. The rails veering away to the right lead to Altrincham. *(T. Noble, David Chatfield Collection)*

Another view of Castlefield Junction, this time looking in the other direction. It is more than a year later and the 'Royal Scot' is in the hands of one of the original 'Peak' class Type 4s, no. D6 *Whernside*, with the Up train on 5 November 1961. The locomotive is passing by the side of Castlefield Junction signal-box and under the main line out of Manchester Central. The MSJ&A lines diverging to the left lead to Altrincham and were used by the electric trains to that Cheshire town as well as passenger trains to Warrington Bank Quay Low Level. *(T. Noble, David Chatfield Collection)*

The location is Ellenbrook, west of Manchester, and another English Electric Type 4, no. D374, is at the head of the Down 'Royal Scot' which has taken the Eccles–Tyldesley–Wigan Springs Branch route in 1961 due to the rebuilding of Weaver Junction. (*Kidderminster Railway Museum*)

The 'Royal Scot' is well off the beaten track as English Electric Type 4, no. D336, heads across Blea Moor with the Down express on Sunday 6 April 1965. Ribblehead viaduct has been left behind while Dent and Garsdale stations are ahead. (*Gavin Morrison*)

Ais Gill is the summit of the Settle & Carlisle line and English Electric Type 4, no. D330, passes the summit with the Up 'Royal Scot' and heads south towards Garsdale on 4 April 1965. In the background is the distinctive shape of Wild Boar Fell. *(Gavin Morrison)*

Endpiece

The 'Royal Scot' was one of three London Midland Region trains with a tailboard, the others being the 'Caledonian' and the 'Red Rose'. At first glance, it is easy to assume that the train has just passed the cameraman, but the truth is that the train is stationary and waiting for a replacement engine. The London-bound train is at Carnforth station on 1 September 1960 following the failure of its train engine, 'Princess Coronation' no. 46223 *Princess Alice*. It will be taken forward by Stanier Class 5 4–6–0, no. 45332. The scene has attracted interest from the waiting travellers on the opposite platform as well as among members of the public on the banking to the right. *(Peter Fitton)*

Acknowledgements

In preparing this book I've received generous help from various contributors and I can say, with honesty, that without such welcomed assistance, completing the task would have been much more difficult.

My grateful thanks go, in alphabetical order, to Hugh Ballantyne, Richard Casserley, Paul Chancellor, David Chatfield, Rex Conway, Doug Darby, Hugh Davies, Peter Fitton, Ron Gee, Tom Heavyside, John Hilton, Barry Hoper, Andrew Ingram, Kidderminster Railway Museum, Michael Mensing, Gavin Morrison, Tony Oldfield, Colin Stacey, Graham Stacey and The Stephenson Locomotive Society, all of whom have been very helpful. My thanks are extended to Cyril Bowker for the kind loan of historical material and to J.B. Mounsey, Tim Shuttleworth, J. Siddall and David Stratton for their offers of assistance.

Various magazines were referred to, including examples from *Trains Illustrated*, *The Railway Magazine*, *Railway World* and *Steam Railway*. The following books were consulted: *Titled Trains of Great Britain* by Cecil J. Allen (Ian Allan Ltd), *Locomotive Headboards* by Dave Peel (Sutton Publishing), and the London Midland Region and Scottish Region books in the series of *BR Steam Motive Power Depots* by Paul Bolger (Ian Allan Publishing).

Last, but not least, I offer my thanks and apologies to my wife, Joyce, and daughter, Helen, for their tolerating the many books, magazines and papers that have been lying around the house over the last few months, reducing the circulation space to an obstacle course on so many occasions.